Screen with a Voice
A History of Moving Pictures in Las Cruces, New Mexico

First Edition

David G. Thomas

Mesilla Valley History Series, Vol 3

For further information, please address
Doc45 Publishing, P. O. Box 5044, Las Cruces, N. M. 88003
books@doc45.com

To obtain printed or ebooks, visit:
doc45.com

Cover artwork by Rose Davis.

ISBN 978-0-692-57680-9

Contents

Mesilla Valley History Series

La Posta – From the Founding of Mesilla, to Corn Exchange Hotel, to Billy the Kid Museum, to Famous Landmark

Giovanni Maria de Agostini, Wonder of The Century – The Astonishing World Traveler Who Was A Hermit

Screen with a Voice – A History of Moving Pictures in Las Cruces, New Mexico

Credits

I thank Elizabeth R. Flores, Library Specialist, New Mexico State University Special Collections, for her invaluable help in locating documents and photos; Chief Travis Brown, Las Cruces Fire Department, for help in identifying the dates of theater fires; and Dennis L. Smith, Geographic Information System Analyst, Doña Ana County Community Development Department, for providing aerial photos of Las Cruces drive-in theaters.

Special thanks to Estella Wilhelm for permitting me to use photos from her personal collection. Estella and her husband Ollie F. Wilhelm managed the theaters in Las Cruces for many years, beginning in 1972. On July 28, 1979, the city of Las Cruces proclaimed "Ollie Wilhelm Day," in recognition of Mr. Wilhelm's generous contributions to the Las Cruces community.

For providing additional photographs and giving me permission to use them, I thank the New Mexico State University Special Collections, the Institute of Historical Survey Foundation (IHSF.org), and Dan Aranda.

Unattributed photos are from the author's collection.

Depicts the world premiere of BILLY THE KID, opening day, October 12, 1930.
Posed in front of the Rio Grande theater are the members of the State College
marching band in military uniform, who gave a free public concert before the first
showing. See page 76 for details. Artwork by Rose Davis.

Preview

Many thousands of books have been written about moving pictures, seemingly covering every conceivable aspect: history, hardware, making films, people in front and behind the cameras, national cinemas, philosophy, sociology, cultural impact. But to the author's knowledge, this book is unique. It covers the history of moving pictures in one town, in the Southwest, from the first showing of a moving picture, to the present.

In this book, the stars are the theaters of Las Cruces. That is not to say that the theater owners and managers – the patrons – the movies – are not covered. They are, and they are important, but they are not the stars.

Like living people, theaters come into existence, age, and – for most – cease to exist. The cause of their death, to use that word, is usually financial abandonment or physical destruction, such as by fire. Sometimes they are resurrected, waking in a new body, in a new location.

A great surprise to the author was the number of long forgotten theaters. They are unremembered no longer. And one, especially, the Airdome Theater which opened in 1914, deserves to be known by all movie historians – it was an automobile drive-in theater, the apparent invention of the concept, two decades before movie history declares the drive-in was invented.

This book begins with a brief history of the invention of moving pictures. Without this backstory, it is impossible to understand how early theater operators secured and exhibited films. The chapters that follow are divided by salient time periods. For example, Chapter Three covers the boom years of 1909 to 1914, when more than 4,000,000 people were viewing movies daily, amounting to over a billion viewers a year.

Movies had arrived as a viable business, and the future seemed to offer movie producers and exhibitors nothing but happy endings. But that would not be the case; changing technology and national events would have a huge impact on the popularity and revenues of the business.

The first projected moving pictures were shown in Las Cruces 110 years ago. Who exhibited those movies? What movies were shown? Since projected moving pictures were invented in 1896, why did it take ten years for the first movie exhibition to reach Las Cruces? Who opened the first theater in town? Where was it located? These questions began the history of moving pictures in Las Cruces, and they are answered in this book. But so are the events and stories that follow.

To supplement this history are 102 photos and illustrations. These include ephemeral documents the author was astounded to find, such as a four-page flyer for Las Cruces' third movie exhibition, at the Rink Theater; historic photos of theaters; aerial photos of drive-ins; and never-before-published photos of the shooting of HANG 'EM HIGH.

Note: This book follows the widely-adopted convention of showing movie titles in all caps. In discussing theaters, the author uses "theater" rather than "theatre." In quotes, the word usage adopted by the source is retained.

Appendix A lists all of the theaters that have existed in Las Cruces – a total of 21 – with critical dates such as day of opening, change of name, change of ownership, remodeling, and, when appropriate, closing. Appendix B lists the movies mentioned in the text.

And now, on with the show....

Chapter 1 | Inventing Moving Pictures – A Brief History

The invention of a viable "moving picture" machine did not require the invention of the idea of making pictures "move." That aspiration had existed even before the invention of photographs in 1839. Various methods of projecting images, with techniques of simulating non-realistic, mechanical movement, known as "magic lanterns," date back to the mid-1600s.[1]

But to make moving pictures using photographs required invention of two separate, but integrated systems of machines. It was necessary to have a machine that could record moving picture content in a functional format and a machine that could make that content viewable.

Peephole Moving Pictures

On May 9, 1891, the American inventor Thomas Edison demonstrated to a convention of the National Federation of Women's Clubs the first moving picture viewing machine, which he called the Kinetoscope.[2] The machine he invented to make pictures for the Kinetoscope he called the Kinetograph.

Edison had originally considered naming his inventions Motoscope and Motograph.[3] Those names sound clunky today, because we are used to semantically sophisticated product names such as iPhone and Wii, but in 1891, such names were part of a long tradition for technical products, and gave the impression of being the latest in technological achievement. For example, commercial versions of magic lanterns that were sold in the decade prior to 1891 were called variously Phasmatrope, Zoetrope, Stereopticon, Choreutoscope, and Kinematoscope. An earlier attempt to create a moving picture camera had been called a Zoopraxiscope.

Edison had been working on a practical moving picture system, which he called a "moving view," for several years prior to 1891. His initial idea for a viewer was to position a sequence of photographs on a cylinder or a disk and then expose them rapidly in sequence to a watcher's eye. In 1889, on trip to Paris, Edison learned of a camera invented by the Frenchman Étienne-Jules Marey, which took a series of photographs on a strip of film.[4] Marey called his invention the Chronophotographic gun.

On his return to his laboratory in Menlo Park, New Jersey, Edison immediately switched to basing his "moving view" system on strips of film. The Kinetograph that he developed over the next couple of years, after numerous failures, recorded 25 pictures a second on a strip of celluloid film 1½ inches wide (approximately 35 mm) and 50 feet long (a rejected, earlier version of the machine used film ¾ of an inch wide).[5]

Although Edison applied for patents in August following his demonstration to the Woman's Club in May, 1891, it was not until April 1, 1894, that he began to sell Kinetoscope machines. In filing for patents, he only filed in the United States, which led to decades of future litigation, as competing motion picture systems were developed and patented in other countries.[6]

The Kinetoscope machine consisted of a four-foot-high wooden cabinet with a peephole in the top, which was the viewing aperture. The box was fitted with a coin mechanism that accepted nickels. When a nickel was inserted into the coin slot, an electric motor inside the box turned on, moving a continuous strip of film past a shutter that opened and closed as each photograph frame was aligned with the shutter. An electric light source illuminated the photograph, which was magnified by a lens. The photographs, moving past the shutter at 40 frames per second, created the illusion in viewers' minds of actual movement.[7]

On April 14, 1894, the first Kinetoscope viewing parlor opened in New York City, with ten machines, earning $120 the first day. Others quickly opened around the country and in Great Britain.[8]

Like the phonograph and records, which Edison had also invented, the Kinetoscope was useless without films to display. The first Kinetograph film was made in 1890 during the development of the camera. This film, entitled MONKEYSHINES NO 1, consisting of a man moving around wildly, can be watched on youtube.com. It was extremely blurry, as was the next film, MONKEYSHINES NO 2.

In 1893, Edison erected the first structure devoted solely to making films – the first film studio. To maximize the availability of direct sunlight for shooting, the structure was built on a circular rail so it could be rotated to follow the sun during the day.[9]

On the release of the Kinetoscope, Edison had less than 20 films available for the machines. Nevertheless, by March 1, 1895, his Kinetoscope Company had made a profit of more than $85,000 on sales of nearly $150,000. But in the following 12 months, the peephole moving picture market fell precipitously, and the company sold just $29,000 worth of product, earning profits of only $4,000.[10]

The decline in sales had two major causes. As noted above, there were not many films to see, and of the ones available, some had far less appeal than others (the perennial film industry problem). And second, there was a newer, vastly more exciting form of moving pictures coming to the market.

Projected Moving Pictures

The advantage of projecting moving pictures over staring into a tiny peephole was obvious to many observers of the Kinetoscope: the experience would be more realistic; more than one person could view a film at once; and it would not be necessary to have ten machines to display ten films, dramatically cutting the cost of film exposition.

The race to produce projected moving pictures resulted in the invention of machines to do that in four countries – France, Germany, England, United States – within about a year of each other.

In France, two brothers, Auguste and Louis Lumière, developed a machine they called the Cinématographe. Their machine was a radical departure from Edison's ideas. The Cinématographe combined the camera to make films and the projector to display the films into one machine; and it was hand cranked, not electric-motor driven. They applied for a French patent for the Cinématographe in February, 1895, demonstrated the machine in a private showing in March, 1895, and had a commercial showing in December, 1895.[11]

In Germany, Max Skladanowsky developed the Bioscope (Bioskop), as he named his projector. The Bioscope was a Rube Goldberg nightmare. It could only display 8 frames a second, which was insufficient for the illusion of motion. To overcome this limitation, the bioscope had two rolls of film, and two sets of eight lenses, and alternated each frame between the two rolls, thus producing 16 frames a second. To make this work, the film had to be cut up and reassembled so that roll one had frames 1, 3, 5, etc., and roll two had frames 2, 4, 6, etc. The bioscope could display films only 48 frames in length (3 seconds of "entertainment").[12]

Skladanowsky received a German patent for the Bioscope in November, 1895, and had a public showing that same month.[13]

In England, Robert W. Paul, who had been taking advantage of Edison's failure to obtain a patent in Great Britain by manufacturing copies of the Kinetoscope for sale there and in Europe, developed a projection machine he called the Theatrograph. The Theatrograph was the first projector to use a gear mechanism to move the film across the light source. This mechanism enabled the projector to stop each film frame in the light for a fraction of a second, before displaying the next frame. One of the peculiarities of the Theatrograph was that the film was collected in a large bag and had to be re-spooled before it could be shown again.[14]

The Theatrograph was demonstrated publically by Paul on February 20, 1896.[15]

Contrary to what one might expect, it was not Edison who developed the first projected moving picture machine in the United States, but rather Woodville Latham, an independent Kinetoscope exhibitor who got the idea of projecting images from some comments his sons made. He began working secretly with William K. L. Dickson to develop a projector. Dickson had done much of the development work for Edison on the Kinetoscope, and he still worked for Edison, so his work with Latham was a clear ethical violation of his employment contract.[16]

On April 21, 1895, the Latham projector, called the Eidoloscope, was demonstrated in the offices of the *New York Sun* newspaper:

> *"This instrument is to the eye what the telephone is to the ear. It annihilates space; it places before the eye incidents that transpired hundreds and thousands of miles distant. It perpetuates action; it makes the dead alive; its resources are wonderful, and words fail to give a comprehensive idea of its magic power."* [17]

The Eidoloscope used film that was two inches wide (shot by a camera of Latham and Dickson's design). It had no mechanism for pausing picture frames over the light source.

Independent of Latham, another group consisting of C. Francis Jenkins and Thomas Armat developed a projector they called the Phantoscope. Jenkins had been working on moving picture inventions for several years when he met Armat, a real estate entrepreneur; the two agreed to form a partnership, with Jenkins contributing his prior inventions and Armat provided financing and assuming responsibility for manufacturing and marketing.[18]

The Phantoscope, an improvement over an earlier, unworkable Jenkins machine, had a mechanism for pausing the picture frame over the light source, like Paul's Theatrograph. It displayed films compatible with the Kinetograph, producing smooth moving pictures.

The Phantoscope had its public launching at the Cotton States Exposition, in Atlanta, Georgia, on September 18, 1895. The debut was not a financial success, perhaps because of competition. Latham was there showing films with his Eidoloscope projector, as was at least one Kinetoscope exhibitor.[19]

Shortly after the Cotton States Exposition showing, Jenkins and Armat made a deal with the firm Raff & Gammon giving that firm world-wide rights to manufacture, rent, and lease the Phantoscope. Raff & Gammon, recognizing the advantages of partnering with the preeminent inventor of the age, approached Edison, and negotiated a deal with him in which Edison agreed to manufacture the Phantoscope and to make films for it. As part of that agreement, the Phantascope was renamed the Vitascope. It was soon being advertised widely as "Edison's Marvelous Vitascope." [20]

The agreement with Edison, in January, 1896, may have been the breaking point, but even before that, relations between Jenkins and Armat were strained. In March, 1896, Armat broke from Jenkins, Raff, and Gammon, and began selling the projector himself, returning to the name Phantascope.[21]

From that point on, both Jenkins and Amat claimed to be the inventor of the Phantascope. This fight between the two men, exceptionally bitter and litigious, lasted for decades. Even as late as 1924, they were still disputing the issue in public. (Jenkins died June 6, 1934, Armat September 30, 1948.) The evidence is that Jenkins invented the initial machine, but Amat contributed ideas, as was recognized by the U. S. Patent Office when it granted them a joint patent in 1897.[22]

In 1893, Elias B. Koopman, Harry N. Marvin, and Herman Casler joined with William K. L. Dickson to develop a moving picture projector they called the Biograph. Dickson, of course, was working for Edison. He was also working with Woodville Latham on the Eidoloscope; so he was hiding his relationship with Latham from Koopman, Marvin, and Casler; he was hiding his relationship with Koopman, Marvin, and Casler from Latham; and he was hiding both of these relationships from Edison.[23]

In November, 1894, the Koopman, Marvin, Casler, and Dickson group, often referred to as K. M. C. D, filed a patent application for the Biograph. In February, 1895, K. M. C. D. filed for a patent for a camera to shoot film for the Biograph, which they named the Mutoscope. They formed the American Mutoscope and Biograph Company to sell the two machines and to produce films.[24]

The Mutoscope used film 2¼ inches wide. Instead of using notches in the film to move the film through the camera, it used a friction feed. Then, when the frame was exposed to the light to produce the image, two punches made holes in the film, marking the location of the frame. The result was a film with unevenly-spaced frames.[25]

1896 – 1897

The years 1896 and 1897 are seminal years for the projected motion picture business. For the first time in human history, moving pictures were being commercially produced and commercially displayed.

These years are also the beginning of a decade of exuberant American entrepreneurism. Distributed electricity was just coming onto the scene, with many large cities installing electric plants. It was also the years of the "War of Currents," between Edison and George Westinghouse, founder of the Westinghouse Electric Company. Edison was doing everything he could to promote direct current (DC) as a standard; Westinghouse was doing everything he could to promote alternating current (AC). The public was being treated to demonstrations by each side purporting to show how their form of sending electricity through wires was superior (and safer) to the other's. (The opening of an AC hydroelectric generating plant at Niagara Falls, built by Westinghouse and Nikola Tesla, eventually won the war of currents.)

Distributed electricity released an unprecedented torrent of inventions. The basic mathematics of electricity was well understood, and manufacturers were producing modular components that could be used to construct all kinds of electrical machines. In this charged atmosphere, moving pictures seemed to offer nearly unlimited money-making opportunities.

In November, 1896, The Phonoscope Publishing Company put out the first trade journal devoted to "sound and sight." As the editor explained in the inaugural issue:

"Our title, 'The Phonoscope,' signifies 'Sound and Sight,' the two senses which add most to our happiness by procuring for us the greatest amount of pleasure and amusement...."

"The talking machines and the different devices for projecting and animating scenes (by means of a succession of views of the same taken at minute intervals of time from each other), all are contrivances for the purpose, as it were, of concentrating sight or sound, and thus to present the quintessence of beauty and pleasure in an agreeable and facile manner...."

"It must appear strange, on that account, that up to the present, the ever awake promoters of trade journals have let this interest pass by without a thought. The individuals and companies engaged in this particular business have each contented themselves with sounding their own praises in order to secure their own particular advantage, totally unmindful of whatever else is of interest to the general public." [26]

Subscription to *"The Phonoscope"* was one dollar per year, or one dollar fifty mailed to a foreign address.

Most of the first issue was devoted to the phonograph, but the section on moving pictures discussed six machines: Vitascope, Cinématographe, Biograph, Eidoloscope, Phantoscope, and Theatrograph.

A column entitled *"New Films for 'Screen' Machines"* listed 22 titles. Samples:

"PIER AND WAVES, taken at Coney Island during the great storm of Oct. 6th, 1896. A tremendous hit."

"LOVE SCENE. Showing lovers, entrance of mother, exit of lover on bicycle. A decided hit."

"FARM SCENE. Feeding of hens and ducks. Unusually fine effects."

"SIDEWALKS OF NEW YORK. This view is taken in Mott street, New York City, and shows a busy throng of people."

"THE OLD GERMAN MILL. In which one of the millers thrusts a woman into the hopper of the mill and she soon emerges from beneath it, having apparently been run through the machinery." [27]

These could be considered the first movie reviews. By the tenth issue, the reviews have expanded to a paragraph or more. A sample from the October, 1897, issue:

"ACROBATIC CLUB SWINGING. Two acrobats in costume assisted by a lady in tights. The latter is seen standing on the shoulder of one of the former from which difficult position she goes through all the intricate movements of club swinging in its different forms. Her supporter is at the same time doing his own exercise with clubs. The third during this time is occupied in grotesquely burlesqueing the actions of his associates. Full of grace and lively action. Very sharp and clear." [28]

Consolidation and Failure

The seemingly bright promise of 1896-1897 darkened in the four years that followed.

Latham's Eidoloscope, as the first machine to display projected moving pictures in public in the United States, appeared well positioned for financial success. And one of the first films the company made for the projector – BULL FIGHT – received widespread public acclaim. The film showed:

"...the charging of the bull at the toreadors and horses, the killing of two horses by the bull and finally the killing of the bull." [29]

But often the Eidoloscope did not work well:

"The machine seemed to be in an ill temper, and the exhibition it gave was short and unsatisfactory." [30]

Latham was soon in financial troubles, and by early 1898, he had sold the patent rights to the machine.

The French projector, the Cinématographe, also did well initially, even dominating the market for much of 1896-1897.

"The firm of Lumière & Sons, inventors of the cinématographe, were obscure, but expert, photographers in Lyons, France, twelve years ago. In 1890 they had prospered so far as to form a stock company of 2,000,000 francs paid

in. Since the invention of the cinématographe a year a half ago, the shares of the company have increased in value over 600 per cent, and the Lumières are rated as millionaires. Their machines are at present being exhibited in several different cities in this country, and the income of the Lumières is stated to be something like $10,000 weekly, with a prospect of its long continuance." [31]

But in late 1897, sales of the Cinématographe and its films began falling off, due to a confluence of causes. Even though it produced superior quality images, its unique film format became a liability as the U. S. industry began to standardize on the 1½ inch (35 mm) format. The company also got into trouble with U. S. customs, as it had brought its projectors into the country as private property to evade custom duties. And finally, it was difficult for a company based in France, making its projectors and almost all its films in Europe, to manage a U. S. operation, leading to, among other problems, employees that could not be trusted:

"...the company discovered that ninety eight films of the positives used in the machine had disappeared and later they found that [employee] Patet had been offering one of the rolls ...to D. Petri Palmeda ...at a price that was much below the real value of the roll."

"The result of all this was that proceedings were taken to have Patet arrested." [32]

The firm best positioned to take advantage of the failure of the Eidoloscope and the faltering of the Cinématographe was the American Mutoscope and Biograph Company. The Biograph, with its mechanism for pausing the frame, produced flicker-free views. The company had Dickson's experience and expertise, as he soon quit Edison and began working full time for the Biograph Company, as it was later called. Dickson built a studio, and like Edison's, it could move to track the sun. The company began churning out films, producing over 250 in 1897, 350 in 1898, and 500 in 1899.[33]

Biograph films, like the films being produced by the industry in general, became ever more sophisticated. In addition to films of locations and news events, gag films and acted films were introduced. The acted films included comedies, dramatic performances, and vaudeville acts. Some of the films portrayed women in suggestive dress or actions.

The Biograph Company's primary competition was the Edison Manufacturing Company. In late 1896, Edison dropped the Vitascope that he had leased from Raff & Gammon, greatly disappointed in its performance, and developed his own machine, the projecting Kinetoscope (or Projectoscope).[34]

Rather than set up his own exhibition operation, as Biograph and Lumière & Sons did, Edison sold projectors and films. He priced his projecting Kinetoscope at $100, less than his competitors, but charged heavily for his films, about 30 cents a foot.[35] And just as he had failed to patent his Vitascope with any government other than the U. S., he failed to set up representative branch offices or companies in other countries. A major problem with the projecting Kinetoscope, which hurt sales, was that the machine ran only on direct current. After several years, Edison had to recognize he had been bested in the Currency War, and switch to AC motors in his projectors.

In the years 1896-1899, when Biograph was leading the industry, Edison produced only about 20 per cent as many films.[36] But, even so, his 1½ film size was becoming the film standard, as it was adopted by other film producers.

Because many of his films were being duplicated and sold (pirated) by unscrupulous dealers, Edison began putting copyright on the films and sending copies to the Library of Congress. The U. S. government did not consider them copyrighted, however, because the law said nothing about "moving pictures" being copyrightable. This lead to a lawsuit by Edison that was finally resolved in the U. S. Federal Courts in 1912, extending copyright protection to all forms of "moving pictures," but not before going through a phase in which the copyright office insisted that to copyright a moving picture, every picture in the film had to be individually copyrighted.[37]

Edison also aggressively pursued patent suits against other moving picture companies, claiming that his patent on the original Kinetograph covered all machines that created moving pictures using "tapes" of film.

Legal expenses were a circumstance none of Edison's competitors wanted. As a result, the smallest of the companies left the business, while the rest negotiated a license agreement with Edison. The sole exception was the Biograph Company, which choose to fight Edison's patent claims.[38]

On July 15, 1901, the U. S. Second Circuit Court of New York ruled that the Biograph Company's Mutoscope took the "substance" of Edison's Kinetograph to create films, and therefore ruled the company was guilty of patient infringement. Given Dickson's role in developing both machines, this was a logical ruling, although Dickson's obvious conflict of interest was not considered by the court.[39]

Recognizing that patent enforcement would put them out of business, the Biograph Company requested a stay of the patent judgment pending appeal, which was granted.[40]

The lower-court patent loss to Edison was a momentous event for Biograph. Their sales deteriorated rapidly, dropping from $134,890 in 1900 to $6,840 in 1901.[41] But on March 10, 1902, the company was saved from probable bankruptcy by a new legal ruling:

"The Circuit Court of Appeals handed down a decision on Monday... reversing a decision in favor of Thomas A. Edison against the American Mutoscope and Biograph Company."

"The Court holds in effect that Mr. Edison didn't really invent the moving picture machine at all. The opinion states that as far back as 1864 a Frenchman named Du Cos made a moving picture machine which was very much like Edison's invention, while Le Prince, another Frenchman, got a patent in this country for a similar apparatus in 1866. Then the Court says:"

"'It is obvious that Mr. Edison was not the pioneer in the large sense of the term, or in the more limited sense in which he would have been if he had also invented the film. But he was not the inventor of the film.'"

"The result of the decision will be that the American Biograph and Mutoscope Company will now actively push the sale of its films, in the sale of

which Edison has had practically a monopoly, and will at once cut the price. Commercially, 20 feet of film, containing photographs to be thrown on a screen, now cost from $7.50 to $10. The Biograph and Mutoscope people propose to sell that film now for $5, or less." [42]

The Biograph Company quickly resumed its position as the leading film producer. In 1903-1904, the company produced 653 new films to Edison's 129.[43] During this same period, the company switched from its 2¼ film format to Edison's 1½ inch format.[44]

Film Censorship

Not surprisingly, moving pictures, from inception, were scrutinized for "moral qualities."

The first governmental body to take action to regulate moving picture content was the State of New York. On February 27, 1900:

"Anthony Comstock appeared before the Assembly Code Committee to urge favorable action on Senator Wagner's bill making it a misdemeanor for any person to have in his possession or exhibit any slot machine or other mechanical contrivance with moving pictures of nude or partly nude female figures."

"Mr. Comstock contended that broad legislation was necessary to stop the picture slot machine evil, which was the ruination of manly youth. His society, he said, had destroyed about seventy-six tons of contraband matter within a short period of time."

"J. T. Easton, representing a mutoscope and biograph company, asked the committee to so amend the bill that partly nude pictures could be exhibited, but not indecent or immoral pictures." [45]

On May 2, 1900, the bill was signed into state law by New York Governor Theodore "Teddy" Roosevelt.[46]

Anthony Comstock, the advocate who appeared before the committee, dedicated his life to battling all and everything he saw as immoral. He was the president of the New York Society for the Suppression of Vice, which he had founded in 1873. He often described himself as *"a weeder in God's Garden."* He claimed, in his long career in suppressing vice, that he had driven 16 people to suicide.[47]

Comstock's tactic in getting censorship laws passed was to carry:

"...a satchel full of lewd, filthy books, pictures, and devices which he spread out before congressmen.... After the law-makers had been regaled with a view of these unclean curiosities, they seemed to be prepared to vote, Aye, on almost any kind of laws for which their vote might be solicited." [48]

Rise of the Nickelodeon

The first use of the word "nickelodeon" appears to be in Boston, Massachusetts, in September, 1888, when a vaudeville theater changed its name from 5 Cent Theater to Nickelodeon.[49] The word was coined by combining nickel and odeon (Greek for theater).

The use of the word for vaudeville theaters quickly spread, being adopted in San Francisco the following month, and in the next several years, widely used for any kind of entertainment hall that charged a nickel, including dance halls.[50]

Following the introduction of moving pictures, vaudeville theaters often added pictures to their shows, but they remained secondary to the live human performances.

In 1906, newspapers began to advertise "Nickelodeons" that showed only moving pictures. For example, the Amuse-U Nickelodeon opened in March, 1906, in Altoona, Pennsylvania.[51] Another early example:

> *"Col. Nickel-O Peters has a 'good thing' at his place of business on South Tyron street. He calls it the 'Nickel-Odeon,' the nickel doubtless referring to the price of admission...."*

> *"The pictures are enjoyable and no one will regret having spent a nickel to see them. Ladies and children will find them especially pleasing. An entirely new set of pictures will be put on tonight, a change being made twice a week."* [52]

These early nickelodeons, and most nickelodeons, were usually not actual theaters with dramatic stages, but just commercial space rented for the purpose of showing moving pictures.

> *"$1,000 will buy an nickelodeon that is a money-maker; good location, cheap rent; fixtures include 100 chairs, picture machine, phonograph.... receipts for the past year averaged $125 per week; net profits for the same time $35 per week."* [53]

Based on these numbers, this nickelodeon was attracting 2,500 paying customers a week.

The idea of a space dedicated just to moving pictures was broadly welcomed by the industry. By 1908, the vast majority of the estimated 8,000 moving picture venues in existence throughout the country were nickelodeons. By 1914, there were an estimated 14,000 U. S. moving picture venues, almost all nickelodeons.[54] But 1914 was the peak year for nickelodeons; the industry began to transition from rented commercial spaces to "movie theaters," structures built specifically for showing moving pictures.

Motion Picture Patents Company

For five years, following the court ruling that Biograph was not infringing on Edison's patents, the two sides viciously competed. It was Edison and most of the smaller movie producing companies, who were paying license fees to Edison, versus Biograph and several foreign producers allied with Biograph.

On November 16, 1907, the Edison side formally organized itself as the United Film Services Protective Association. The purpose was to establish enforceable control of all moving picture production and distribution not associated with Biograph. The rules required that films be rented only from Association members, films not be duplicated, films not be sub-rented, films not be sold second-hand, and displayed films be returned to the producer.[55]

Biograph quickly decided that one big jolly monopoly would be in its interest too. In December, 1908, the two sides formed the Motion Picture Patents Company. The members brought together under one controlling legal structure all of the existing U. S. patents for moving picture production and display. Also cheerily joining was Eastman Kodak, the maker of nearly all of the film stock used in the U. S.

The obvious economic benefit of the Patents Company to its members was to fix the price of films at a level that would have been impossible in a competitive environment. The film exhibitor had to "take it or leave it."

In addition to price control, the production monopoly enabled the producers to force exhibitors to take all of the films they produced, or get none. This solved the "quality" problem – for every good or popular film there were many not so good and not so popular – and exhibitors wanted only the good and the popular, or at least the ability to choose. This tail-wagging-the-dog phenomena established by the Patents monopoly in 1908 remains dominant in the industry today, where distribution tightly controls what films end up in the theaters, and for how long.[56]

Busting the Patents Monopoly

Edison and Biograph, and the smaller producers who joined the Patents monopoly, had tight control of the industry for a couple of years, but then they began to face "independents." These were exhibitors who managed to obtain films in two main ways: from the few producers who were not members of the Patents monopoly, and from exhibitors who had signed with the Patents Company, but were willing, when paid sufficiently, to duplicate films or otherwise violate the company's rules.

To fight this prohibited behavior, the Motion Picture Patents Company hired undercover inspectors and imposed strict penalties on Patents violators.

In 1911, William Fox, owner of the Greater New York Film Company, sued the Patents Company, alleging it was an illegal monopoly as defined by the Sherman Antitrust Act of 1890. In July, 1912, the court issued a preliminary ruling.

"There is a 'moving picture trust,' according to William Fox, who has brought suit in behalf of the Greater New York Film Company, in the U. S. District Court, charging that the Biograph Company, the Edison Manufacturing Company, the Essanay Film Manufacturing Company, the Kalem Company, George Kleine, the Lubin Manufacturing Company, the Pathé Frères Company, the Selig Polyscope Company, the Vitograph Company of America, and the Melies Manufacturing Company, which manufactures the great majority of moving picture films in this country have formed a holding concern, the Motion Picture Patents Company and a distributing company, the General Film Company, to control the industry."

"Judge Hand granted an injunction on Saturday expressing the belief that there was an unlawful combination, and the action against it under the Sherman Act will be heard before a special examiner."

"The ten moving picture concerns... formed the Motion Picture Patents Company in 1908, and gradually cut down the number of film agencies from 140 to 70. Then, in order to get the distribution business as well as the manufacture into its own hands, he says it formed the General Film Company. Instead of selling its films outright as it had done before to the agents, it merely leased them, charging as much for the rental as for the purchase and forcing the return of the films they had already bought... and inserted a clause in the agreements by which the agents had to return any film on fourteen day's notice." [57]

Fox had become an Edison moving picture exhibitor in October, 1904. In the years that followed, he became the biggest exhibitor in New York City, owning numerous theaters, including three on Broadway, each seating several thousand patrons.

Fox had accepted the constraints of the Patents Company. But when the same agents formed the General Film Company to buy up the moving picture distributors, known at the time as "exchanges," Fox rebelled, refusing to sell his exchange. In retaliation, the Patents Company refused to provide his theaters with films.

The injunction ruling in Fox's lawsuit meant that the Patents Company had to provide films to Fox's exchange until a final decision was issued by the court. Recognizing the high likelihood of an ultimate loss on the issue, the Patents Company settled out of court with Fox, permitting him to obtain and distribute their films.[58]

But the loss in Fox's lawsuit was small compared to what came next. In August, 1912, the U. S. Government filed an antitrust lawsuit against the Patents Company. The legal proceedings between the two parties dragged on until October, 1915, when the case was decided for the U. S. Government.[59] But by that time the Patents Company was already an empty shell and the movie business was open to all who cared to start a company.

Photos

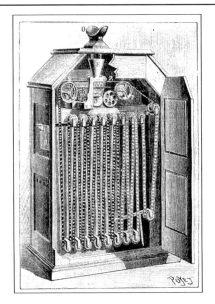

Edison's peephole Kinetoscope.

Ad for Edison Projecting Kinetoscope, *Reel Life, A Weekly Magazine of Kinetic Drama and Literature,* Vol III, No 1, inside cover.

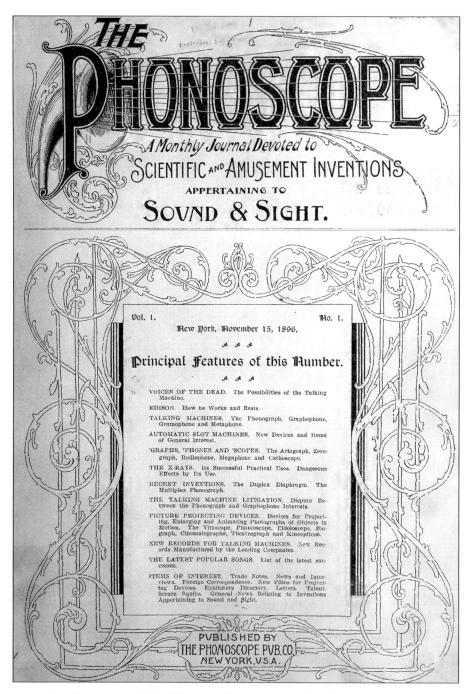

The Phonoscope, A Monthly Journal Devoted to Scientific and Amusement Inventions Appertaining to Sound and Sight, 1896, Vol 1, No 1, cover.

Chapter 2 | Moving Pictures Arrive in Las Cruces

Moving pictures arrived in Las Cruces late – ten years late.

El Paso

That was not true for El Paso, Texas, 45 miles south of Las Cruces. On April 21, 1897, the city was given its first ever exhibition of projected moving pictures (exactly one year to the day after the first public demonstration of projected moving pictures in the United States):

> "The Buckman Farce Comedy company arrived this morning and will open tonight at the opera house in 'Wife Wanted.' Ladies when accompanied by an escort with a full paid ticket will be admitted free...."

> "The Magnescope (sic), a better machine than the Vitascope or the Projecting Kinetescope (sic) will be put on between the acts by the company during the week, beginning Wednesday night." [1]

The Magniscope was one of the short-lived projectors developed in 1896. The inventor, Edward Hill Amet, designed it specifically for travelling theatrical companies. It used the 1½ inch film format, was notably lighter than the other projectors, and used burning lime as a light source.

The public's response:

> "The novel feature of the show was the animated pictures shown by the magnescope and the loud applause each production received showed they were pleasing to the audience. The first picture produced was a scene in a blacksmith shop; the next was the Empire express train running at the rate of 70 miles an hour; the next scene was a lone fisherman sitting on the end of a plank, a mischievous fellow removes a rock from the other end of the plank and the fisherman falls into the water and then throws water on the man who causes the trouble and the scene ends by the latter picking up the heavy rock and throwing it into the water at the fisherman; the next scene was the serpentine dance giving all the colors in the dancer's dress; the last scene was the New York fire department going to a fire on Broadway, lead by the chief. This scene was a natural as possible for it to be, showing the crowds on the thoroughfare getting out of the way of the different fire apparatus as they came down the street."

> "The audience left well pleased with the night's entertainment." [2]

These are Edison films. For example, the dance film was A SERPENTINE DANCE and featured the, at the time, well-known performer Annabelle Whitford. The film had been made in 1894.[3] Evidently, it had been hand-colored, as many early films were.

Burning lime was especially dangerous in an exhibit setting:

> *"'Living pictures' are exhibited very generally throughout the country, and here are some of the names by which they are designated: The motograph, cinématograph, animatoscope, animatograph, projectoscope, cinématoscope, vitascope, veriscope, viveoroscope, ravoscope, magnoscope, cinégraphoscope, and living photographs. By whatever name known they present one of the most dangerous fire hazards introduced of late years.... The destruction of the Charity Bazaar in Paris and the loss of 124 lives were due to a cinematograph exhibition. Since then there have been so many other fires... that the authorities have prescribed stringent regulations for such exhibitions."*

> *"How the thing works is thus described by an expert operator of living photographs:"*

> *"'Just before passing the last picture of a rather long series through the cinematograph, the limelight, for some reason, became accidentally extinguished. It was the work of a moment, of course, to press a match against the still incandescent lime and so kindle the gas lantern, after which I placed that match carefully in the tray of the lantern. Underneath the table on which the instrument stood was a pile consisting of sufficient celluloid film to reach to the top of St. Paul's Cathedral.... Suppose that, as might easily have happened in the almost excusable flurry of the moment, that match had been dropped on the floor. In an instant that heap of film would have been in a hissing blaze of frightfully hot flame, high enough to reach the ceiling and broad enough to lick the wall and fire anything inflammable within a yard or two.'"* [4]

The second appearance of moving pictures in El Paso was eight months later, December 27, 1897, when the Bittner Theatre Company arrived for a week's engagement:

> *"Tonight the play will be Out of Darkness and between acts the company will produce pictures from Edison's latest improvement on the Vitascope.... The prices are 25, 35 and 50 cents, but all ladies accompanied by escorts will be admitted free."* [5] (See the flyer at the end of this chapter for a list of films shown.)

The third appearance was March 21, 1898, when the Edna Paige Company toured El Paso:

> *"Supported by their own company of 12 people. Singing and dancing specialties, and Calcium light effects. Edison's vitascope, presenting life-size animated pictures of a Spanish bull fight, and Corbett and Fitzimmons' Carson City prize fight."* [6]

Edna Paige (Potts) died 13 months later, of consumption (TB). She was 23 years old.[7]

On October 15, 1898, moving pictures were shown for the first time in El Paso as stand-alone entertainment:

> *"Tonight the best Vitascope ever exhibited in El Paso will give a performance at Mayer's opera house. The machine is of French patent and is far*

ahead of the American make, the picture being a great deal plainer. There is not as much flickering to it, consequently the eyes are not strained in watching the pictures." [8]

The French "Vitascope" referenced is the Cinématographe.

In August, 1899, the El Paso newspaper published a long article entitled *"Moving Picture Possibilities: The Astonishing Things a Cinematograph Expert Predicts."* After explaining how various special effects were accomplished, such as disappearing people or objects, the quoted expert, Mr. Robert Pitard, noted the rapid improvement in film technology:

"Formerly a film fifty feet long was the practical limit; now 500 feet is nothing remarkable. Then, again, it was thought necessary to take at least forty pictures a second, and most people still suppose that is the rate. It has been found, as a matter of fact, that the same result may be obtained in most cases with fifteen pictures a second, and at present that might be called the standard speed." [9]

Beginning in 1900, moving picture exhibition in El Paso becomes relatively common, although still as an accompaniment to a touring company.

On November 13, 1905, El Paso secured its first theater intended to be primarily a moving picture theater, the "Lyric."

"The Lyric Theater opened last evening to a large and appreciative audience. It being the first night, everything did not work quite as smoothly as it will tonight and hereafter, but the many present seemed to enjoy the performance and went away feeling that they had spent a very pleasant evening."

"The bill for this week is a good one, and as popular prices prevail a large audience should be on hand. Hereafter there will be special matinees Wednesday, Friday, Saturday and Sunday, at which the admission will be only 10 cents and 15 cents." [10]

The Lyric was converted from an older stage theater, the Chopin Hall, and continued to feature some vaudeville acts.[11] Its primary draw was moving pictures, however.

Within a short time, a number of other moving picture theaters opened in El Paso, including the Bijou, Crawford, Franklin, Star, Palace Picture Parlor, and Wigwam.

The Wigwam Theater had the oddest history. Built originally as the Fashion Saloon in 1880, it was the most famous gambling hall in "the great southwest." It was also the site of the first electric light installed in El Paso.

"The owners, wishing to eclipse all other rivals, purchased an individual lighting plant in New York, and established it in the back yard of their place, hiring an old Southern Pacific engineer to run it. This was the event of the year and people came for miles to see the wonderful light that did not smoke or go out o'nights." [12]

In October, 1907, the *El Paso Herald* noted:

> *"The people have money. Just stand outside a moving picture show some evening and watch them crowd in. There are now nine of these shows running in El Paso, with two vaudeville theaters and the 'road house' and none of them have gone bankrupt or wailed about hard times."* [13]

A danger constantly associated with moving picture theaters was fire. In July, 1907, the El Paso city council passed an ordinance regulating the use of electricity in moving pictures venues, designed to prevent fires:

> *"Unless the proprietors of every moving picture machine in El Paso complies with the electrical code of the National Board of Fire Underwriters within 48 hours, the places of business will be closed."*

> *"Notice to this effect was served on the proprietors of the moving picture shows yesterday afternoon at 5 o'clock by city electrician Arthur Samworth...."*

> *"The code provides for certain wiring and also a magazine for each reel on the machine for celluloid films. The moving picture machines in El Paso are without the two magazines for the films and it will be impossible for the proprietors to secure such within the time limit."* [14]

The ordinance required that the floors and walls of moving picture venues be lined with sheet iron, and that the projector and operator be situated at the rear of the venue and be enclosed within a fire-proof booth.

Six months after the passage of the ordinance, the reporters of the *El Paso Herald:*

> *"...visited scores of fire traps that are made to take the place of theaters. In the great majority of the places visited little pretext of meeting the ordinary requirements of the law is made...."*

> *"...at times the places are packed so that there would be no other result than death to many in the audience if one of the machines should take fire, as the machines are all located in front of the house and would start a fire that would cut off the people from the exits."* [15]

Las Cruces

The first showing of moving pictures in Las Cruces was January 22, 1906, courtesy of the Franklin-Huston Orpheum Show, *"traveling in their own special car, direct from the Eastern Houses and on their Pacific Coast Tour."* The pictures were shown between acts. The engagement was for one night only:

> *"Las Cruces Theatrical Patrons can congratulate themselves on having the Franklin-Huston Orpheum Show, Monday night. They play El Paso Saturday night and had a date open between El Paso and Albuquerque, so they decided to give it to us.... They should be patronized and it may help us to get a good company once and a while."* [16]

The editor's wish to get a good company once and a while was answered just ten days later (February 2), when the Dixie Carnival arrived for a 3-day engagement. Beside the standard fare, the carnival showed MEET ME AT THE FOUNTAIN, WANTED A DOG, and THE GREAT TRAIN ROBBERY.

THE GREAT TRAIN ROBBERY, an Edison film produced and shot by Edwin S. Porter in 1903, is often praised as the most significant film made up to that date. It was a narrative film, shot on location, with camera movement, double-exposure, and cross cutting. Cross cutting enabled the film to tell two parallel stories. The most famous scene in the film showed the leader of the train robbers, in a close-up, pointing and firing his gun directly into the camera. Shot separately, the scene could be put either at the film's beginning or end, however the exhibitor decided.[17]. The film was *"enthusiastically applauded"* by Las Cruces viewers.[18]

The next appearance of moving pictures in Las Cruces was July 27, 1907, when a travelling exhibition company opened a four-day engagement at the Rink Theater.

> *"The pictures are said to be much better than any ever shown here.... You will enjoy them if you go."* [19]

The Rink Theater had been built in 1885 by Albert Eugene Van Patten as both a dramatic playhouse and a skating rink (hence the name).

> *"The skating rink he is building... is ready for the roof. The building is one of the largest for the purpose in the Territory. It is 60 feet wide and 160 feet long, and has eight windows on the side.... It will also be used as a hall; a large stage will be erected in the east end, and it will be seated with chairs."* [20]

The presentation the first night was a live play followed by the Millar Brothers Diorama, a mechanical lantern show:

> *"This, without a doubt, is the most ingenious production which mechanical skill has ever been able to present. It is a distinct novelty from beginning to end and one of the richest things extant, including reproductions of the great paintings and wonderful transformations."* [21]

The show the second night consisted of 17 French-made films. The first feature was YE HAUNTED WAYSIDE INN, directed by Marie Georges Jean Méliès:

> *"This production is certainly magnificent in its weird realism. It is a succession of marvelous surprises and startling visions, introducing many new tricks and novel effects."*

Méliès had been a professional magician before he began directing films, and his films were the first to introduce many camera special effects.

The third night presented a different assortment French-made films; the evening's main feature was THE CHIMNEY SWEEP, produced by Lumière & Sons:

> *"The film is 1200 feet in length – 25 thrilling scenes – duration about 28 minutes."*

The presentation the final night consisted of comedies, location productions, and a historical film, THE FINDING OF AMERICA. (See the Rink Theater flyer at the end of this chapter for a list of the films shown.)

So why was Las Cruces so much later than El Paso in getting moving pictures?

The answer is that the city of El Paso got electricity in 1896, but Las Cruces did not get electricity until March, 1905.[22] [23] (The electrical plant in El Paso was alternating current; the one in Las Cruces direct current. In December, 1908, the Las Cruces Electric Light Company switched to alternating current.[24])

No city electricity meant that exhibitors had to bring their own power generator to run their projectors, which, it appears, was an effective obstacle to establishing a permanent Las Cruces moving picture venue.

In February, 1908, a second permanent venue opened in a backroom of the Ideal Grocery store, *"giving as good an exhibition as can be seen in any of the large cities."* [25] It called itself the Vaudette Moving Picture show and offered a special Saturday matinee to school children; within a few months it was out of business.[26]

In May, 1908, the Electric Theater established itself in the Armory Building. The first planned showing had to be cancelled, because the *"films that they intended to use fail[ed] to arrive in time."* The company promised shows on Tuesdays, Thursdays, and Saturdays. Admission was ten and fifteen cents.[27]

By June 27, 1908, The Electric Theater was doing well enough to run an advertisement in the Las Cruces newspaper:

> *"A first-class performance is guaranteed. Don't fail to come. It will be a pleasure to everyone."* [28]

The Electric Theater was soon to get serious competition. On February 2, 1909, Courtland O. Bennett and Park R. Birdwell opened the Wonderland Theater:

> *"A high-class moral entertainment furnished nightly, with complete change of program three times a week.... Moving pictures are no novelty, but the grade of class shown at the Wonderland is a surprise that is highly appreciated by amusement seekers. Matinees Saturdays at 2:30 o'clock."* [29]

The Las Cruces newspaper called it:

> *"...the home of refined amusement, the pictures being the world in motion. Comedies, tragedies, farces and travelogues are reproduced in life-like form in these wonderful films. All the features of the regular theater find their counterpart in the photographic theater. You can always learn something: you can always be amused and often uplifted and inspired by the wonderful productions."* [30]

The Wonderland Theater was an outdoor theater. It consisted of a high wall surrounding the accoutrements of a moving picture venue: screen, projector, and chairs. The wall prevented those outside the wall from seeing the pictures. The theater could seat 300 and employed four workers. As an outdoor venue, the Wonderland was only able to give shows in the summer.[31]

Shortly after being christened Wonderland Theater, Bennett changed the theater's name to Airdome.

In July, 1909, Bennett formed a partnership with the owners of the Electric Theater, J. W. Rapier and G. E. Warren. The Electric Theater was renamed the Grand Theater. The partners announced that:

"They will give their shows at the Airdome as long as the weather permits; and on wet days as the Grand Theater."

"Heretofore both shows have given more than their money's worth and hereafter they promise to give even better service." [32]

Photos

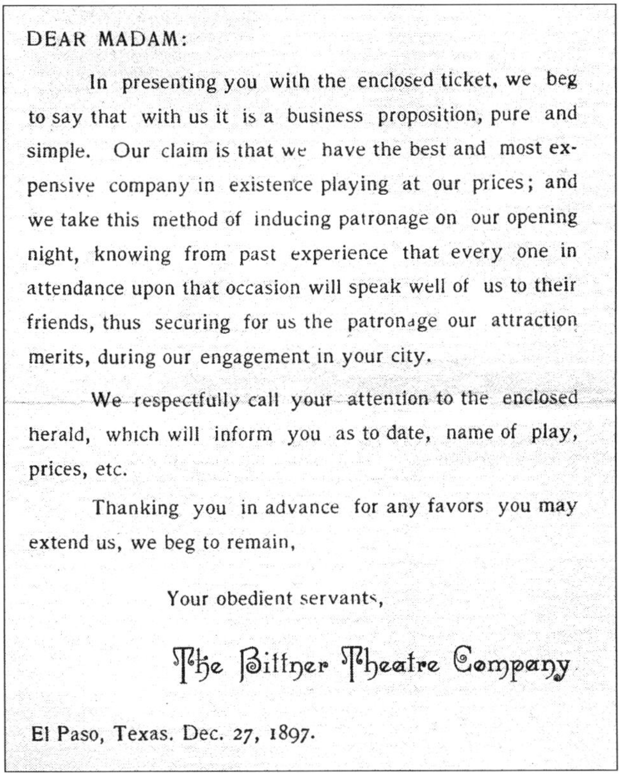

DEAR MADAM:

In presenting you with the enclosed ticket, we beg to say that with us it is a business proposition, pure and simple. Our claim is that we have the best and most expensive company in existence playing at our prices; and we take this method of inducing patronage on our opening night, knowing from past experience that every one in attendance upon that occasion will speak well of us to their friends, thus securing for us the patronage our attraction merits, during our engagement in your city.

We respectfully call your attention to the enclosed herald, which will inform you as to date, name of play, prices, etc.

Thanking you in advance for any favors you may extend us, we beg to remain,

Your obedient servants,

The Bittner Theatre Company

El Paso, Texas. Dec. 27, 1897.

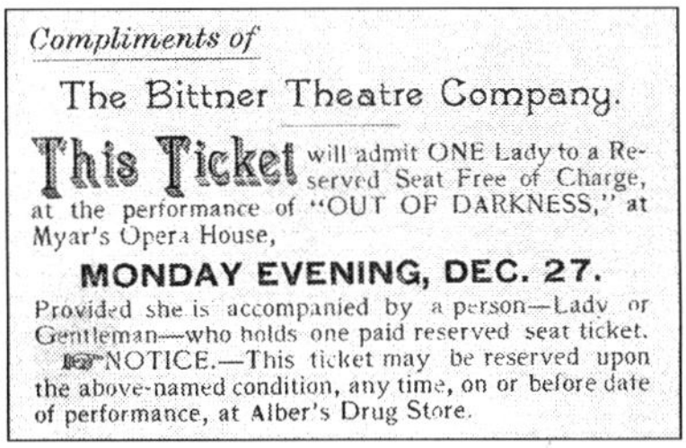

Compliments of

The Bittner Theatre Company.

This Ticket will admit ONE Lady to a Reserved Seat Free of Charge, at the performance of "OUT OF DARKNESS," at Myar's Opera House,

MONDAY EVENING, DEC. 27.

Provided she is accompanied by a person—Lady or Gentleman—who holds one paid reserved seat ticket. NOTICE.—This ticket may be reserved upon the above-named condition, any time, on or before date of performance, at Alber's Drug Store.

Invitation and ticket for Bittner Theatre Company performance in El Paso, Texas, December 27, 1897, the second ever showing of films in El Paso. Courtesy Archives and Special Collections, New Mexico State University.

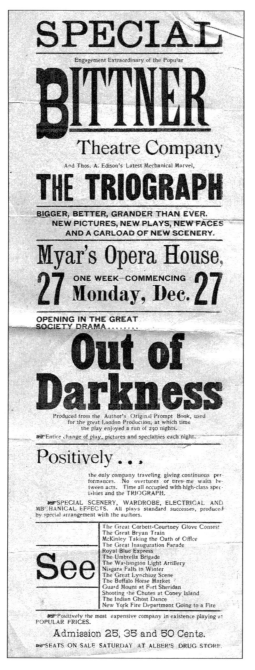

Flyer for Bittner Theatre Company performance week of December 27, 1897. The company was using the Triograph projector, a machine manufactured by Lumière & Sons and designed to use Edison's 1½ inch format. The company was showing almost all of the available Edison films. Courtesy Archives and Special Collections, New Mexico State University.

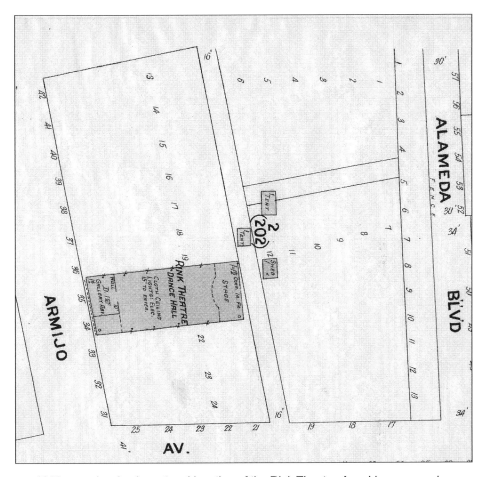

1908 map showing layout and location of the Rink Theater. A residence occupies the site today. The block is bound on the north by W. Hadley Ave., south by W. Court Ave., east by N. Alameda St., and west by N. Armijo St. 1908 Sanborn Fire Insurance Map of Las Cruces, Library of Congress.

Nearly Two Million People

HAVE SEEN THE

Great DIORAMA

Can You Afford to Miss It?

AMERICA'S GRANDEST

The FAMOUS

DIORAMA

In the Latest

PICTORIAL PRODUCTIONS

An Attraction that Charms the Mind and Stirs the Imagination

The Attraction that Pleases — Great in its own Greatness

The Only Picture Attraction that has Become Famous

NOT THE ORDINARY

—

SOMETHING EXTRAORDINARY

TO THE PUBLIC

IN PRESENTING this announcement of the famous DIORAMA, we wish to modestly call your attention to our past promises and performances. The exhibition has always been of the highest order and has given the best of satisfaction. We are proud of this, and the encouragement we have received from the public has inspired us to greater efforts and we now promise you the best and most complete exhibition of Triple Dissolving Mechanical Dioramas, Wonderful Moving Pictures and Pretty Illustrated Songs in the word.   Respectfully,

THE MANAGEMENT.

YOU SHOULD TAKE ADVANTAGE OF THIS OPPORTUNITY

IN CONJUNCTON WITH CLUB DRAMATICO NEO-MEXICANO

ONE NIGHT ONLY

IN THE RINK SATURDAY 27 APRIL

Prices: 25 Cents and 50 Cents

Flyer for four-day picture show exhibition at Rink Theater, Las Cruces, April 27, 1907. Program for the first night, the third ever showing of films in Las Cruces. Courtesy Archives and Special Collections, New Mexico State University.

AN ATTRACTION TO CHARM THE MIND

GEO. MELIES GRAND PARISIAN FANTASTICAL PRODUCTION

Yᵉ HAUNTED WAYSIDE INN

In Twelve Scenes — Very Comical and Mysterious

This production is certainly magnificent in its weird realism. It is a succession of marvelous surprises and startling visions, introducing many new tricks and novel effects. It will please all, for they are numerous who like impossibilities in hobgoblins. The subject is developed in good taste and w ll cause you to laugh as you have never laughed before.

PICTURES THAT PLEASE

TURNING THE TABLES. Mr. Policeman decides to make things interesting for a number of boys, but the boys get the upper hand and give Mr. Policeman a most exciting experience. Excruciatingly funny.

CLIFF SCENERY AT THE GOBBINS. One of the most beautiful scenes in Ireland and nothing like it in any other part of the world; magnificently grand.

MILAN CATHEDRAL. A pretty picture of the far-famed cathedral. As the scene changes to a moonlight view, the cathedral is illuminated. A charming picture with beautiful color effect.

GLIMPSE OF VENICE. In this we present five representative views of Venice—the entrance to the grand canal, beautiful Venetian architectures, St. Mark's and the Doge's Palace, St. Mark's square and its curious sights, and a grand circular panoramic view of the grand canal. A very pretty subject.

CRYSTAL PALACE MYSTIFICATIONS—the prettiest of all mystical pictures. The conjurer and his assistants appear amid the most beautiful scenery, and after performing some of the most marvelous feats in magic, disappear as mysteriously as they appeared. A most gorgeous subject developed in the best of good taste.

YOUTHFUL ROBBERS. One of the most exciting comedy chase pictures yet produced. A continuous scream of laughter.

MONTE CARLO, MONACO. A circular panoramic picture, showing the beautiful palm gardens and many of the grand buildings. The last part shows the grand entrance to the Monte Carlo Casino, the world's greatest gambling resort, with great swarms of people entering and leaving the building. Very fine scenically and architecturally.

STREETS OF JERUSALEM. An interesting scene taken in Jerusalem's busiest section. Shows the natives in their picturesque costumes going in all directions. As the camera revolves, a herd of camels is seen on the way to Mt. Zion, which is plainly visible.

SCENES IN SICILY. A delightful picture of typical interest, showing Sicilian women and children at their work. A very pretty subject.

MEPHISTO'S SCHOOL OF MAGIC. A mystical picture that is really wonderful, introducing many tricks that are entirely new. A picture that will keep you guessing from beginning to end.

THE ASTRONOMICAL DREAMER. A mysterious picture replete with comical situations; the astronomer has fallen asleep over his studies and in his dream the interior of the observatory and all its contents become animated, and many wonderful changes take place. It will cause the most sober-minded spectator to enjoy a hearty laugh.

THE RAPIDS OF KILLARNEY. A very pretty picture of the world-famed rapids just after a heavy shower, showing boats passing up and down stream, and the surrounding scenery—beautiful beyond description.

THE TARGITEERS. This is one of the funniest motion pictures yet produced. A young city chap and his sweetheart have a most exciting experience which leaves the audience convulsed with laughter.

LAKE GENEVA. A beautiful scene showing the old Castle of Chilon in springtime and changing to a winter view, the lake frozen and snow falling. The coloring is exquisitely grand; it is a picture to charm the mind.

CHASED BY HOUNDS. This is the funniest of all the funny comedy chase pictures yet produced—one continuous roar of side-splitting laughter.

The Most Gorgeous and Artistic Exhibition in the World

PATHE'S GORGEOUS PARISIAN PRODUCTION

𝒯he CONJUROR'S LOTTERY

The Prettiest Parisian Mythological Production that has yet been offered. The color effect is very pretty. A beautiful subject developed from the early Peasantry—As played in the Robin Hood Theatre of Paris.

In this pretty series of six motion pictures we present one of the most beautiful mythological pictures ever shown. It is a succession of very pretty scenes, with an abundance of simple, innocent, wholesome comedy that leaves the audience convulsed with laughter. "The man who laughs at night returns to his daily toil rejuvenated."

AN ATTRACTION THAT STIRS THE IMAGINATION

Rink Theater Flyer, Las Cruces, April 27, 1907. Program for second night. Courtesy Archives and Special Collections, New Mexico State University.

Rink Theater Flyer, Las Cruces, April 27, 1907. Program for third night. Courtesy Archives and Special Collections, New Mexico State University.

AMERICA'S GRANDEST PICTURE ATTRACTION

The Greatest of all Pictorial Comedy Successes

THE COUNTRY FAIR

IN 12 COMIC SCENES
ONE CONTINUOUS SCREAM OF LAUGHTER

¶ In this pretty series of twelve motion pictures we present one of the most beautiful comedy productions that has ever been shown. It is a succession of fascinating comic scenes with an abundance of wholesome comedy that leaves the audience convulsed with laughter.

BRADSHAW'S
MOVING
PICTURES
HAVE NO EQUAL

You Must
See
This Big
Display

A LONG ...
AND
NOVEL
PROGRAM

The Most Gorgeous Production

THE SCENIC GRANDEUR
OF
ITALY

IN 26 PRETTY SCENES

The Most Magnificent of all Moving Picture Scenic Productions

Beautiful Electro-Polytint Color Effects

NOTHING LIKE IT EVER ATTEMPTED BY
POET OR PAINTER

THE SCENES

The Gondolas in Venice, Beautiful Venetian Architectures, Entrance to the Grand Canal, Circular panorama of the Grand Canal, St. Marks' Square, The Doge's Palace, City of Naples, Mt. Vesuvius, Mouth of the Crater, Streets of Capri, Bay of Biskra, Beautiful Tivoli, Modes of Travel, Stereoscopic panorama from electric railway, The great cable incline, Ancient Rome and the ruins, Modern Rome, Street scenes in Rome, St. Peter's Cathedral, The Vatican, The Colonades, Circular panorama of the Colosseum, Circular panorama of the Arena, Forward panorama of the Bridge of Sighs, Moonlight on Lake Mgoire, Water jousting at Genoa.

BRADSHAW'S
FAMOUS
DIORAMA
GREATER THAN EVER

Nothing
TO OFFEND

Refined,
Polite
AND

Moral in Tone

LAUGH
AND BE
MERRY

The Grand Historical Production

THE FINDING OF AMERICA

A FANTASY ON EARLY HISTORY

IN 15 PRETTY SCENES

A Beautiful Subject with Rich Costumes and Most Elaborate Settings. A Most Extraordinary Production, with Very Pretty Scenic Effects. Thrillingly Interesting from the Educational Point of View as well as from the Amusement Side.

GREATER AND GRANDER THAN EVER

Rink Theater Flyer, Las Cruces, April 27, 1907. Program for final night. Courtesy Archives and Special Collections, New Mexico State University.

Armory building. Site of the Electric Theater, 1908-1911. Undated photo. Courtesy
Archives and Special Collections, New Mexico State University.

Chapter 3 | Business Flourishes – 1909-1914

"While 10,000,000 persons paid admission to baseball games in the record breaking season of 1908, the moving picture show draws an audience of 4,000,000 daily, a total attendance of more than a billion a year or an average of one visit a month to this form of amusement for every man, woman and child in the whole country." [1]

This report on the state of the moving picture industry was published in U. S. newspapers in May, 1909. The article noted further that to supply the more than 7,000 moving picture venues in the country, the industry produced over 190 miles of film each year. New York City had more than 500 moving picture outlets.

The article noted:

"...the most significant and interesting phase of the moving picture show... is the revolution it has brought about in providing entertainment for the masses at their very doors."

"Instead of millions of people having to go to the moving picture show, it has come to them."

"The ease of access makes them very convenient and popular; from one to a dozen are to be found within a short walk of almost any part of the larger cities. The moving picture exhibitor does not have to go to the expense of constructing a theatre. His equipment is so simple that all that is necessary is to rent a store or hall." [2]

This praise for next-door accessibility and the simplicity of starting a moving picture business was written just as the Nickelodeon phase of the industry was reaching its zenith and the next phase was beginning: custom-built movie theaters.

Custom-built theaters with lofty ceilings, sloped floors, and large screens offered a far more pleasant moving picture viewing experience than folding chairs in a rented store front. And as many editorial writers noted, small venues were particularly unhealthy:

"Dr. A. H. VanDyke, a member of the police board, [stated] that some of the rooms in which moving pictures shows are given are breeding places for disease."

"I have seen places that have been made out of small rooms that have both ends closed up so that fresh air cannot circulate. Men are allowed to spit on the floors and dirt and dust accumulates. The small electric fans only keep the impure air moving about... so that the air one person breathes is fanned into the lungs of some one else." [3]

The first important custom-built theater, which became a model for subsequent picture theaters, was the Montgomery, in Atlanta Georgia:

> *"...only recently opened, which is considered to be in many respects the most perfect appointed moving picture theater in the world. The interior reproduces a great hall of the Tudor period of English architecture, the groined roof harmonizing with the presence of the largest pipe organ in any theater in America. The screen upon which the pictures are shown is erected just in front of the organ, the pipes showing above it. There are a dozen private boxes, a balcony, rest room for women, and many other attractions and advantages. This theater is hailed as the type of the city moving picture show of the future."*

> *"There is a distinct opinion in the moving picture trade that the ordinary store show will decline in popularity with the multiplication of specially constructed exhibition houses."* [4]

Such lavish theaters were called picture palaces.

Las Cruces Still a Backwater

But just as moving pictures were late to arrive in Las Cruces, so were custom theaters. The two firms that joined forces in July, 1909, continued to be the only sources of moving pictures until October 13, 1911, when it was announced that two new picture companies were coming to town:

> *"Las Cruces will soon have three picture shows where it has had but one. The Robinson drug store building will be occupied by the Higashi motion pictures, and J. R. Givan of El Paso has his large concern moving here now except the chairs which are on the way. It is not settled yet where this business will locate...."* [5]

The new exhibitors were welcomed by the Las Cruces newspaper, because *"the people of our town have needed some entertainment of this sort as there is practically no place to go in the evenings."* [6]

A couple of weeks later, Frank Higashi announced the establishment of the Crystal Theatre in the Mitchell Building on Main Street:

> *"Mr. Higashi the proprietor, has been in the business for many years, and is informed on all the latest and most attractive features available of this class of amusement. The accommodations will be comfortable and satisfactory to all patrons."* [7]

The Crystal Theatre, at the corner of Main Street and Organ Avenue, had its formal opening on November 11, 1911. [8]

The owners of the Airdome and the Electric Theaters responded to the new competition by renaming the Electric Theater the Bijou, and by remodeling the Airdome, making it more comfortable and installing a large water tank with an electric motor to pump water in the case of fire. [9] Their advertisements in the Las Cruces paper offered *"combination tickets, good for both the Bijou and Airdome Theaters,"* for 15 cents. [10]

The promised third company, to be launched by J. R. Givan of El Paso, never opened.

Pictures Made in Las Cruces

On February 16, 1912, the Las Cruces newspaper noted that Powers Moving Picture Company was in the area making moving pictures.

"We have in Las Cruces... a company of mountain climbers, mesa riders and play actors as we nightly watch at the moving picture shows. They have come to New Mexico direct from New York for the purpose of studying everything of interest obtainable in this part of the country – the scenery, climate and different peoples that they daily study will hold many attractions and lessons for the company for further work and reference."

"The Powers company has fifteen ladies and gentlemen, each an experienced specialist in his or her department." [11]

The Powers Moving Picture Company was owned by Nicholas Powers, the inventor of a film projector called the Cameragraph. Operating under the patent protection of the Motion Picture Patents Company, Powers had built the first Cameragraph in 1908. He continued to refine the machine in the years that followed, and for several decades his machines were one of the two or three movie projectors that dominated the industry.

After scouting scenes, the Powers Moving Picture Company decamped to W. W. Cox's ranch on the east slope of the Organ Mountains. There they filmed a number of movies, including two described in some detail in the newspaper:

In the first film, rustlers riding from the Isaacs' ranch, located on the west side of the Organ Mountains, steal a herd of cows from Cox's ranch after overpowering the cowboys guarding them. In driving off the cattle, the rustlers encounter an automobile driven by a wealthy contractor, who they rob. When the sheriff learns of the two crimes, he organizes a posse, which leads to a wild chase through a mountain pass and to the eventual capture of the rustlers. Numerous locals had roles in the movie, including Las Cruces sheriff Felipe Lucero, who played the sheriff, and W. W. Cox, who played the ranch owner.

The second film, a romance, was more complicated. An American lady flees to the Cox Ranch to avoid the unwanted attentions of a wealthy Englishman. When he follows her there, she asks for protection from the Cox ranch hands. The ranch hands do all they can to drive him off, but he is insuperable. The final scene:

"...is a realistic round-up and branding scene.... After branding a number of calves, Cox orders the Englishman from the place and demands that he desist from his attentions to the lady. He is roped, dragged from his horse and turned over to the cowboys with branding irons. When escape is found impossible and there is no other alternative... he yields and signs a contract releasing the young woman and promising immunity from further annoyance." [12]

Crystal Theater Changes Hands

In October, 1912, Higashi sold the Crystal Theater to Roline E. Banner, who had operated a commercial photography business in Las Cruces since 1898.[13] [14] Banner immediately solicited the public's help in renaming the theater:

> *"$10.00 cash for a name for Banner's new photo-play house. Full particulars at ticket office."* [15]

Evidently a better name was never suggested, as the name was not changed.

Las Cruces' first custom built theater was announced on July 29, 1913:

> *"A contract has been let to the Bascom-French company for a one story brick building to be erected on the lot on Main street owned by E. D. Williams. The building will be thirty two feet wide by one hundred long. A part of it will be used for a barber shop and part for a moving picture show."* [16]

Emory Douglas Williams, a prominent black citizen, earned his living as a barber. He owned considerable property in and around Las Cruces, including the Star Barber Shop on the lot where the theater was to be erected.

In September, 1913, Banner opened his new theater in the new building:

> *"Banner, the Crystal Theater man, is fitting up a first class play house for moving pictures in the Lohman building on Main Street. Fine film will be shown in this place at slightly advanced price. The Crystal will continue the same pictures as before. This will be an interesting experiment and one that should interest all who love good pictures and fine artistic effect."* [17]

Williams also moved into the new building, renaming his business the Antiseptic Barber Shop.[18]

In late November, 1913, the Banner Theater, as the new theater was being called, showed one of the spectacular run-away hits of 1912, SIEGFRIED, based on Richard Wagner's opera and produced by the Ambrosia Company of Italy, *"whose studios and surroundings have the advantage of having the finest equipment of scenery and natural surroundings in the world."* [19]

Within a few months, the Banner Theater was renamed Star Theater.

In April, 1914, the Star Theater showed the 1913 smash hit QUO VADIS, based on the book by the Nobel Prize winner Henryk Sienkiewicz. The film was eight reels long, one of the first films of that length, lasting two hours and an intermission. The producer was the Cines Company of Italy. The title is Latin for "Where are you going?" understood in the slang sense of "What's happening?"

Critics at the time almost universally agreed that QUO VADIS was the best film ever made:

> *"It is in no sense an exaggeration to say that 'Quo Vadis' is by far the greatest picture ever shown.... The spirit of this book is faithfully portrayed, even in the smallest details; the acting is one of the very best and the scenery, reproduced from the very localities about which the book was written, is superb in its beauty and accuracy."*

"Historically and morally, the picture is in the highest degree educational and elevating. The corrupt life of Rome under Nero is shown in startling vividness and the growth of the Christian religion in the days of its martyrdom is portrayed with careful attention to historical details. The scene at the burning of Rome is one of the greatest ever caught by the moving picture camera." [20]

In June, Banner opened a new outdoor theater on south Main Street, calling it the Open Air Picture Show. [21]

Drive-In Theater Invented

In response to Banner's new Open Air Picture Show, the owners of the now five-year-old Airdome decided to close it and build a new Airdome at a new location:

"Work began Monday on the new open air theater of Bennett and Birdwell, adjoining the Masonic Temple on the west and facing on Griggs street. The theater will be fenced solidly eight feet in height, and will be cozily seated, with a stage and other convenience for the business and its patrons. **An automobile drive will hold two rows of cars permitting their occupants to see the performance without leaving the cars.** *"* [22] (Bold added by author.)

The new Airdome opened July 11, 1914. The opening notice provided more details on the construction of the theater.

"The new Airdome has a capacity of 450 and has room to park ten cars. The curtain is sixteen feet square and is high enough to be seen from all parts of the theater." [23]

A number of articles, books, and web sites relay how the drive-in theater was invented in 1933 by Richard Milton Holingshead, Jr. And it is true that he received a patent on May 16, 1933, for *"a new and useful outdoor theater... whereby the transportation facilities to and from the theater are made to constitute an element of the seating facilities of the theater."* [24]

Clearly Holingshead was not the inventor of the drive-in movie theater. That honor apparently goes to Bennett and Birdwell and their new Airdome Theater. In surveying contemporary newspapers in New Mexico and surrounding states, the author was unable to find another account of a moving picture theater accommodating patron viewing from automobile seats (or *"transportation facilities"* as Holingshead had it). If this does not establish Bennett and Birdwell as the inventors of the concept, it certainly confirms them as one of first to do so, overturning eight decades of received moving picture history.

Airdome

The word Airdome for naming an outdoor theater was apparently used for the first time in El Paso in May, 1906:

"Over 1000 people filled the enclosure at the east side of the city hall – the Airdome, the new summer pleasure resort, for its opening performance last evening...."

"The Airdome is a large enclosure with a roof garden and bleacher feature, and a large level garden space directly in front of the stage for chairs and tables...."

"Everything is finished in white and the place is very attractive and is clean as a pin." [25]

The next use of the Airdome name was in September, 1908, when an open-air theater in Tucumcari, New Mexico, was so designated.[26]

In February, 1909, the Wonderland Theater in Las Cruces was renamed Airdome, as noted earlier, apparently the third use of the name.[27]

Albuquerque, New Mexico, received a large Airdome outdoor theater in May, 1911:

"The dreamland of the west is that theater beautiful, the Airdome; opening Thursday night, May fourth."

"A big double orchestra will give nightly concerts. This amusement enterprise has twenty-eight people on their pay roll...." [28]

In May, 1914, construction began on an outdoor theater in on Deming, New Mexico, the city's first, to be called Airdome. The builder announced the theater would be *"one of the finest open air houses of entertainment in the southwest."*

"The lantern [projector] that will be used in the airdome will be the latest on the market and will be specially adapted for outdoor shows, while the screen will also be of a special make that has always given best results in open air theaters and that will not be liable to cause a strain on the eyes, as so many screens do." [29]

"The seating capacity of the Airdome will be 500 and the seats will be so arranged that people in all parts of the house will be able to see the pictures without having their view impeded by the heads of the persons in front of them, which will be a great and welcome change for the short people who have the misfortune sometimes to sit behind some broad shouldered six-footer or behind some lady with a wide hat." [30]

All of these Airdomes had different owners – but the owners all had an identical problem. During the summer months an indoor theater could be outrageously hot, often above 90 degrees. An outdoor theater after dark would generally be cooler. The downside of outdoor operation was bad weather and the constantly changing time of sunset, making a year-round, fixed starting time impossible.

An example of bad weather at the Las Cruces Airdome:

"Though the thunder crashed and the lightening flashed, and the rain came down in torrents, the audience stuck for the finish, taking refuge in cars and under the operating shed." [31]

Except for the Airdome in Las Cruces, none of these Airdome's had spaces to watch movies while sitting in a car, further strengthening the argument that the drive-in was invented at the Airdome in Las Cruces.

An Innovative Promotion

On December 1, 1914, the Star Theater announced the showing of the first install-ment (episode) of THE MILLION DOLLAR MYSTERY.[32]

THE MILLION DOLLAR MYSTERY was based on a novel by Harold MacGrath, a well-known, successful novelist. The film consisted of 22 installments. Each week, a new installment was to be shown, until the twenty-third week, when the final, climatic installment would be shown.

But the final installment and the climax were unmade and unknown. Instead, the movie advertisements promised, in large letters, that the *"man, woman or child who writes the most acceptable solution"* to the story's ending will win $10,000 and that ending will be shot as the final installment.[33]

An unknown ending, and a prize for the person who invented that ending, might seem intriguing enough, but the movie producer had another hook to catch viewers: the chapter text of the novel on which each installment was based was published in the local newspaper on the same day the installment was shown. Thus, viewers could read the novel in conjunction with seeing the film.

The story of THE MILLION DOLLAR MYSTERY revolved around the efforts of a secret society, known as the Black Hundred, to steal a million dollars from a rich heiress. The events of the story included:

> *"...the fall of a balloon in mid-ocean, the death-defying portrayal of a rail-road wreck... [and] scenes of the ocean bottom's mysterious life and vegetation – pictures taken under water at tremendous expense."* [34]

Miss Ida Damon, a 24-year old living with her elderly parents in St. Louis, Missouri, won THE MILLION DOLLAR MYSTERY ending contest. The newspaper, in reporting her win, described her as:

> *"Five feet tall, almost plump, athletically poised, clear skinned, home grown complexion, brown hair and eyes to match."* [35]

In a follow-up interview, Damon revealed that after the announcement of her win, she received 1,742 proposal letters in the mail. She selected ten that she corresponded with, eventually settling on J. Arthur Painter, *"a railway mail clerk of Chicago. She liked his style of writing."* After *"one or two visits"* they became engaged and shortly thereaf-ter, married. She used $4,000 of her winnings to buy her parents a new house.[36] [37]

THE MILLION DOLLAR MYSTERY was one of the first of the "serials," as this kind of episodic film was soon named. THE MILLION DOLLAR MYSTERY earned over a million dollars for its production company, Thanhouser Film Corporation, and inspired a sequel, THE TWENTY MILLION DOLLAR MYSTERY, a spoof, THE TEN BILLION DOLLAR VITAGRAPH MYSTERY, and many copycats.[38]

Photos

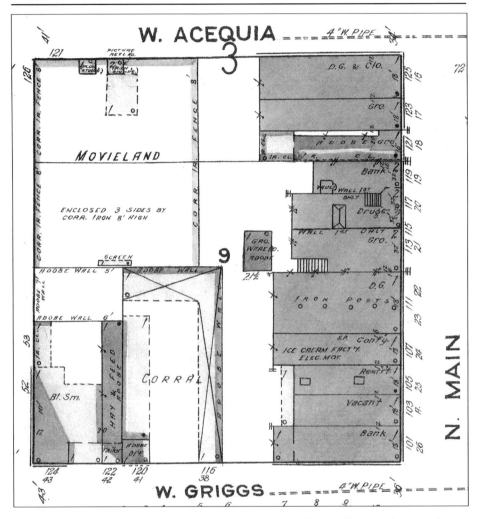

1921 map showing layout and location of the new Airdome Theater (renamed Movieland in April, 1920) – <u>the world's first drive-in theater</u>. The open air theater is enclosed on 3 sides by corrugated iron fencing eight feet high. The block is bound on the north by W. Organ Ave. (W. Acequia then), south by W. Griggs Ave., east by N. Main St., and west by N. Water St. The site today is occupied by the Zeffiro Pizzeria Napoletana restaurant and its parking lot. 1921 Sanborn Fire Insurance Map of Las Cruces, Library of Congress.

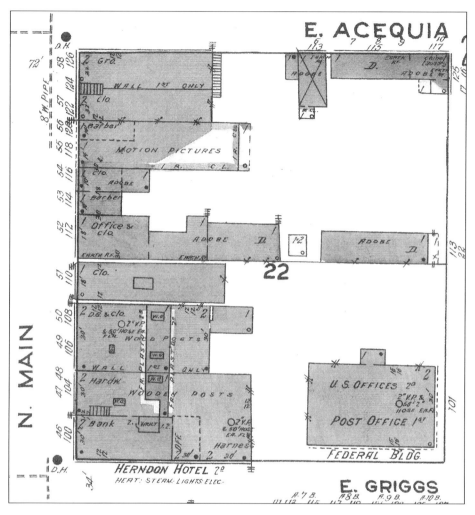

1921 map showing layout and location of the Banner Theater (renamed Star in January, 1914). The map shows Emory Williams' barber shop in the north-west corner. The block is bound on the north by E. Organ Ave. (E. Acequia then), south by E. Griggs Ave., east by N. Church St., and west by N. Main St. The site currently is an empty lot. 1921 Sanborn Fire Insurance Map of Las Cruces, Library of Congress.

Open Air Picture Show flyer for the film JUDITH OF BETHULIA, directed by D. W. Griffith, based on a poem and play by Thomas Bailey Aldrich. The film starred Blanche Sweet and Henry B. Walthall. The film is historically significant, as it was the first feature-length film made by the Biograph Company. After making the film, Griffith left Biograph with his entire company of players, so the film was not released until 1914.

The story is based biblical Book of Judith. During the siege of the Jewish city of Bethulia by the Assyrians, Judith, a widow, disguises herself as a harem girl and goes to the enemy camp. There she succeeds in inducing the Assyrian king to dismiss all his servents, and when he is overcome with wine, she takes his sword and cuts off his head.

"Among the striking scenes in this remarkable picture are those showing the battle outside the city, the assaults on the massive walls, the scenes of famine within, the unsuccessful attempt of the Jews to regain the walls, the tragic death of [king] Holofrenes at the hands of Judith, and the final destruction of the Assyrian camp." Courtesy Archives and Special Collections, New Mexico State University.

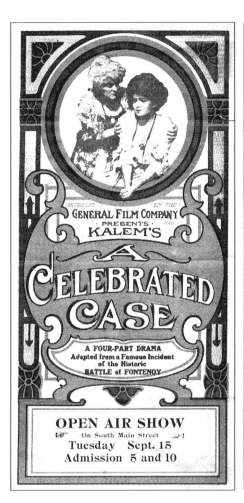

Open Air Picture Show flyer for the 1914 film A CELEBRATED CASE, produced by the Kalem Company. The film starred Alice Joyce, Guy Coombs, and Marguerite Courtot. The film was four reels, lasting about 50 minutes.

The story is based on an incident that occurred at the 1745 Battle of Fontenoy, during the War of the Austrian Succession. A daughter, unaware that she has been mislead, testifies that her father has murdered her mother. Her father is sentenced to the galleys for life. The daughter eventually discovers that her testimony was false and her father innocent. Twelve years later the daughter encounters her father, who after a series of events, is able to prove his innocence and attain his freedom. Courtesy Archives and Special Collections, New Mexico State University.

Official Herald

THE
MILLION DOLLAR MYSTERY

Thanhouser's Million Dollar Motion Picture Production

Herald No. 3   Episode No. 3

AGAIN THIS KEEN
MIND GUESSES

⫸WIGWAM⫷
SAT. OCT. 3   MAT. 3 PM

Wigwam Theater (El Paso) flyer for episode 3 of THE MILLION DOLLAR
MYSTERY. The serial was directed by Howell Hansel and starred Florence
La Badie, Marguerite Snow, and James Cruze. See the chapter text for a plot
description.

Chapter 4 | War Years – 1915-1919

The assassination of Archduke Franz Ferdinand of Austria, heir to the Austro-Hungarian throne, on June 28, 1914, is considered by historians to be the day World War I began, although nobody at the time understood the monumental consequences – certainly not in Las Cruces where the assassination received no mention in the local newspaper.

On July 28, 1914, Austria-Hungary declared war on Serbia; on August 1, Germany declared war on Russia, and two days later, declared war on France and invaded France through neutral Belgium. On August 5, the Las Cruces newspaper commented on the war for the first time:

> *"What is the trouble [!] in Europe all about? Briefly, it has its source in race prejudices: the Slave peoples, numbering 130,000,000 and including the Russians, Bulgarians, Poles, Bohemians, Serbians, and many smaller groups, have a strong race feeling for each other, and resent attempted domination by other great groups of the Aryan family, such as the Teutons and Celts."* [1]

By the end of August, the major European powers and Japan had declared war on Germany and Austria-Hungary, and Germany and Austria-Hungary had reciprocated.

As the United States had declared itself neutral on August 4, the first 16 months of the war had limited direct effect on lives in the United States. In Las Cruces, war news was reported in the newspaper, but with little feeling of personal threat and with the view that the war was something distant – and something to stay the heck out of.

A New Theater Company

On April 16, 1915, the newspaper announced a new theater entrant:

> *"W. P. Stevenson of the Wade Amusement company, which is promoting a new and up to date open air theater, arrived here this morning to take charge of advertising for the entertainment feature which goes into the new theater. The public of Las Cruces have their eye on the new amusement place and are waiting anxiously for its opening, which will take place in about 10 days."*

> *"The policy of the theater is to give the best first run pictures that money can secure, and to furnish good music and occasionally vaudeville of high character. A beautiful dancing floor of hard maple has been laid in the auditorium of the theater of which dances will be given a certain nights in the week."*

> *"The Wade theater is well built and will serve as well in bad weather as in good weather, being well roofed and yet entirely open and airy. Seven hundred people may be comfortably seated in the auditorium. Automobile entrances and places for 40 or more cars within the theater grounds and in-line position to see the pictures and witness all performances on the stage is a feature of the place that will please car owners. A border of green lawn will enclose the theater*

proper and the auto drives will frame this in on either side. The theater entrance will be electric lighted and bright as day." [2]

The theater was roofed, but open on the sides. It had space for 40 or more cars to be positioned to watch the show, making it another example of a historically early drive-in theater.

On April 23, the new theater, calling itself the Theatre de Guadalupe, announced its grand opening, with an advertisement touting *"A dollar show for 10 and 15 cents"* and *"Plenty of room for your auto, drive in."* [3] The accompanying newspaper article noted:

> *"The contest is open to hand in a name for the new theater. Say, you! Who's going to win the ten [dollars] offered as a prize for the name for the no-name theater. Get busy."* [4]

The grand opening of the "no-name" theater was a huge success:

> *"The crowd was the largest picture show crowd ever seen here, as every seat was taken and standing room all filled. The car parks were literally jammed with loaded cars and altogether the picture, the fine service of the open air management, and the splendid crowd were fine evidence of the interest the entire people take in really good pictures."* [5]

Eighteen days later, on May 11, the "no-name" theater advertised using its new name, De Luxe Theater, for the first time. No one was given credit for suggesting the name. The ad noted: *"plenty of room for your auto."* [6]

The same issue of the newspaper reported the sinking, on May 7, of the British ocean liner *RMS Lusitania* by a German U-boat. Of the 1,959 aboard, 1,198 were killed. Just prior to the sinking, the Germans had announced a new sea policy in which it claimed the right to sink the civilian ships of its enemies. The newspaper editor expressed the opinion of most Americans:

> *"This last massacre violates all previous law of the seas. It accords with the law of the seas recently promulgated by the German government and announced by it in American newspaper advertisements a week ago today – the morning on which the Lusitania sailed."* [7]

Consolidation and Turnover

On June 29, 1915, Birdwell's partner Bennett sold his portion of their Star and (new) Airdome theaters to Banner. The new partnership of Banner and Birdwell then bought the De Luxe Theater from the Wade Amusement Company. That made Banner and Birdwell the owners of all of the theaters in Las Cruces: the Star, the Open Air Picture Show, the Airdome, and the De Luxe. [8]

By consolidating, Banner and Birdwell eliminated what must have been costly competition between themselves. They immediately closed the Open Air Picture Show, not needing three outdoor theaters.

On January 21, 1916, Banner and Birdwell sold the Star and Airdome Theaters to J. H. Hanford and Elbert B. Curtis, who promised *"the Las Cruces public will get the best in motion pictures at all times."* [9]

Hanford's and Curtis's first action in delivering on their promise was to move the Star Theater into a new facility, the Samuel Bean Building, located on the east side of Main Street, near the corner of Main and Organ Avenue.[10] (The old Star building became a garage.) Then in March, they remodeled the Bean Building, adding a 25 foot extension and increasing the seating capacity by 100 chairs. *"This change is made necessary by the large attendance at this popular place of amusement."* [11]

In May, Curtis bought out Hanford, becoming the sole proprietor of the "nicest little theaters" in the southwest. He opened the Airdome, which had been closed for the winter, and announced a policy in which the Star Theater would be open only when the weather was too bad to attend the Airdome. Hanford left to *"enter electrical work in which he is an expert."* [12]

On June 13, Birdwell, with a new partner, A. F. Katzenstein, announced the re-opening of the De Luxe Theater, under the new name Pastime Theater. [13]

Two weeks later, June 30, Curtis sold the Star and Airdome theaters to Birdwell and his brother Parke Birdwell. Katzenstein is not mentioned, so it is unclear what happened to his partnership with Birdwell. Curtis left for El Paso, *"where he expects to enter business."* Now owning the Star and Airdome, Birdwell closed the just opened Pastime Theater. [14]

So, in a thirteen month period (May, 1915 to June, 1916), the theaters of Las Cruces changed hands four times. This suggests the theaters were not making reliable profits, even though the newspaper reported good attendance. During this period, moving pictures were better than they had ever been, and business nationally was excellent. But the moving and remodeling of the Star, and the seasonal switching between outdoor and indoor theaters, suggests recognition by the owners that the venues were not sufficiently appealing to patrons. Various reports in industry publications during this period list a number of problems with small theaters: outdated projectors, inexperienced operators, insufficient screen illumination, a dirty screen or a poor quality screen, poor ventilation, and poor quality films.[15] It is possible that Las Cruces theaters had some or all of these problems.

On July 7, 1916, the Las Cruces city council passed an ordinance authorizing the censorship of moving pictures:

> *"...any person may make complaint to the trustees at any time on the obscenity, immorality or the suggestion of either of these in any picture shown in Las Cruces."*

> *"A board of censors will be appointed to view any such picture and report to the city council when any such adverse report shall have been made."* [16]

The justification of the ordinance was that *"some suggestive pictures have appeared from time to time."*

An example of a film that could have lead to this ordinance was HYPOCRITES, shown at the Airdome:

> *"Hypocrites has probably been the subject of more newspaper and other comment than any other play now presented in the American stage. In New*

York it was approved by the Chief of Police, a committee of clergymen and councilmen. In Chicago so much criticism was aroused over the play that it was forbidden. In El Paso the play was presented to crowded houses...."

"...two women, Margaret Edwards as the principal actress, and Lois Weber as author and producing director are responsible for the film's excellence." [17]

In the film, a naked Edwards plays the part of a mythical symbol, Naked Truth. A minister, disappointed with the religious sincerity shown by his parishioners, has a dream-like mystical encounter with Naked Truth. Naked Truth continues to appear as the story develops, until the climax, in which the minister is stoned to death by a mob of (as we have learned) hypocrites. The scenes in which Edwards appears naked are double exposure scenes, so she always looks ghostly and somewhat out of focus. (Several scenes from the movie can be seen on Youtube.com.) [18]

Lois Weber, the director, was one of the few female writers and directors working in the industry during this early period. Margaret Edwards was considered an extraordinary beauty, having won an international contest as the "perfect woman" at the age of fourteen.[19]

With the Las Cruces theaters under a single ownership, newspaper ads for the theaters became tiny, and were often missing. An exception occurred December 1, when a large advertisement appeared for THE BIRTH OF A NATION, a movie that is praised still by critics for its innovative techniques. The tag lines read:

"The most stupendous Dramatic Narrative ever yet unfolded on any stage since the world began."

"Its dynamic force has electrified the world."

"Millions have seen it. Go see it yourself." [20]

The ticket prices were raised from the usual 15 and 25 cents to 50 cents, 75 cents, one dollar, and one dollar fifty, and seats could be reserved. The movie was shown in the Star Theater.

World War I Declared

On April 6, 1917, the United States declared war on the Germany and its allies. There were numerous reasons why the United States decided to go to war, but the proximate cause was that Germany had started sinking U. S. Merchant Marine ships.

If you imaged that the Las Cruces newspaper announced the war with a screaming three-inch headline, "WAR DECLARED!," you would be wrong. The April 6 issue of the paper does not discuss the upcoming war. Instead, mixed in with articles of local interest, such as the story of a man who lit a match to see how much gasoline was in his car's gas tank, while holding the gas pump filing hose (with bad results), is an article praising the speech President Woodrow Wilson gave to Congress requesting the declaration of war:

"The president's message is a great state paper which will rank in history among the great state papers of which Americans in future years will be proud." [21]

In the issue just before war was declared, the newspaper has an editorial in which the writer takes a remarkably detached stance toward the possibility of war.

"The people of the United States generally are standing loyally by the president. Some of us believe he has acted with too much deliberation and some of us believe he has acted too fast, but all of us agree that he is a patriot and that his judgment usually is clear and trustworthy. Besides, he knows the facts as we cannot know them." [22]

After the declaration of war, the U. S. government quickly recognized it could use the regular gathering of audiences at theaters to help the war effort. Government films were released that promoted buying Liberty Bonds, explained rationing, price controls, and the new draft law, and praised citizens and businesses for doing their share to win the war.

In August, the government implemented a policy of paid and volunteer speakers giving a four-minute speech on war issues before each moving picture:

"The idea originated with the president of the United States, and it is by his authority that a campaign of education is to be carried on in every moving picture house in the country." [23]

In October, the government passed a comprehensive revenue law that increased existing taxes and put new taxes on goods and services that previously were untaxed. A tax of one cent per linear foot was placed on film production; a tax of one cent per ten cents was placed on moving picture tickets.

"The tax on a 10 cent admission is one cent; on a 15 cent admission, two cents; on a 20 cent admission, two cents; and on a 25 cent admission, three cents. [24]

The Las Cruces newspaper noted:

"It has been many years since pennies have been used in this section of the Southwest, but the war demands that the little red boys be put back in to circulation again." [25]

"The war is introducing the humble penny into California. For the first time in the history of the state it will be used in commerce." [26]

In November, 1917, Emil Brutinel bought the Star and Airdome theaters from Birdwell.[27] Two months later, he had an accident:

"Emil Brutinel of the Star Theatre had the misfortune to get his thumb caught in the cogs of the machine at the theatre and lost the tip of one of his thumbs." [28]

On the same day, Brutinel learned that his 19-year-old cousin had been killed in action in France.[29]

In April, an advertisement for the Airdome touted its "coolness" for the first time:

"The coolest place in town to spend your evenings. Drive right in with your car, enjoy the best of silent drama."

"...sit in your upholstered seat and enjoy an evening's recreation." [30]

There may be an unspoken message in this advertisement. By April, 1918, it was public knowledge that the world was suffering from an influenza epidemic – an epidemic that would eventually kill three to five percent of the world's population (50 to 100 million). An unusual characteristic of this particular flu strain was that it killed healthy adults disproportionately more than had previous strains, which had mostly killed the young, elderly, and sick.

Fear of getting the flu led to a large drop in theater attendance, with some cities ordering theaters closed.[31] Attending a movie at an outdoor theater, sitting in your own car, would tend to mitigate against the fear of being infected due to being seated next to someone in a closed, poorly ventilated room.

World War I Ends

On November 11, 1918, an armistice, forced on Germany and its allies by military defeat, was signed between the two warring sides, ending the war. Although the Las Cruces newspaper did not break out a large headline from its presumed stash, it did have a long front page column on the ending of the war. The column reported that there were spontaneous celebrations all over town, and that no business was being conducted as people were *"too excited and enthusiastic to attend to business."* [32]

In the evening, at a county-wide celebration organized by city leaders, a mock trial was held of the deposed leader of Germany, Kaiser Wilhelm II, in which he was convicted of brutal war crimes and sentenced to death.

In real life, the Kaiser fled Germany to exile in the Netherlands, whose ruler, Queen Wilhelmina, refused to extradite him for trial. British Prime Minister David Lloyd George and French President Raymond Poincaré argued strongly for extradition, but U. S. President Wilson opposed it. Wilhelm II wrote his memoirs and lived a life of leisure in comfortable exile. When Hitler came to power, he tried to promote his son into the position of German Kaiser (emperor), but with no success. He died June 4, 1941, 643 days after Germany started World War II by invading Poland.

Photos

Star Theatre flyer for the 1914 film JULIUS CAESAR, produced by George Kleine.
Courtesy Archives and Special Collections, New Mexico State University.

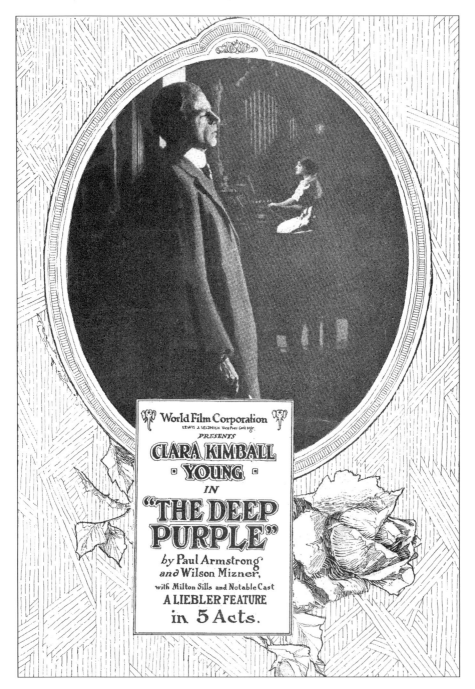

(New) Airdome Theatre flyer for the 1915 film THE DEEP PURPLE, produced by Peerless Productions. Courtesy Archives and Special Collections, New Mexico State University.

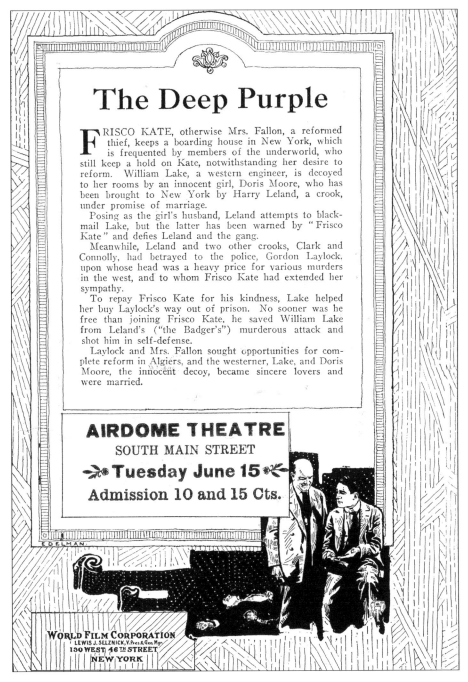

The Deep Purple

FRISCO KATE, otherwise Mrs. Fallon, a reformed thief, keeps a boarding house in New York, which is frequented by members of the underworld, who still keep a hold on Kate, notwithstanding her desire to reform. William Lake, a western engineer, is decoyed to her rooms by an innocent girl, Doris Moore, who has been brought to New York by Harry Leland, a crook, under promise of marriage.

Posing as the girl's husband, Leland attempts to blackmail Lake, but the latter has been warned by "Frisco Kate" and defies Leland and the gang.

Meanwhile, Leland and two other crooks, Clark and Connolly, had betrayed to the police, Gordon Laylock, upon whose head was a heavy price for various murders in the west, and to whom Frisco Kate had extended her sympathy.

To repay Frisco Kate for his kindness, Lake helped her buy Laylock's way out of prison. No sooner was he free than joining Frisco Kate, he saved William Lake from Leland's ("the Badger's") murderous attack and shot him in self-defense.

Laylock and Mrs. Fallon sought opportunities for complete reform in Algiers, and the westerner, Lake, and Doris Moore, the innocent decoy, became sincere lovers and were married.

AIRDOME THEATRE
SOUTH MAIN STREET
❧ Tuesday June 15 ☙
Admission 10 and 15 Cts.

WORLD FILM CORPORATION
LEWIS J. SELZNICK, V. Pres. & Gen Mgr.
130 WEST 46TH STREET
NEW YORK

THE DEEP PURPLE flyer, second side. Courtesy Archives and Special Collections, New Mexico State University.

(New) Airdome Theater flyer for the 1918 film EYE FOR EYE. Courtesy Archives and Special Collections, New Mexico State University.

SOMETHING ABOUT THE PLAY FOR

"Look me in the eye."

"**E**YE FOR EYE" is a mighty drama transferred to the screen, starring peerless Mme. Nazimóva. A picturization of the play "L'Occident," by the great Belgian dramatist, Kistemaeckers, it shows the vital difference between the ideals of the Occident and the Orient. Nazimova plays Hassouna, a wayward rose of the desert, who is true to her own ideals of right and wrong. But those ideals are not those of the French officer, Captain Cadiere, to whom honor and love of his country's flag represent the highest good. Scenes of the greatest brilliancy and dramatic value are shown in the desert, in Tangiers, in the French circus where Hassouna becomes a dancer, and in the Captain's villa on the Bay of Marseilles. "Eye for Eye" is a screen triumph no one can afford to miss.

AIRDOME

EYE FOR EYE flyer, second side. Courtesy Archives and Special Collections, New Mexico State University.

Chapter 5 | The Twenties – 1920-1925

On January 17, 1920, it became illegal to buy "intoxicating liquors" to drink for pleasure in the United States.

To have the legal authority to ban drinking alcohol, it was necessary to amend the U. S. Constitution. The amendment that achieved this, the Eighteenth Amendment, was approved by the last of the required 36 states on January 16, 1919. The amendment made it legal for Congress to make a law banning the manufacture, transportation, and sale of intoxicating liquors, which Congress obediently, in anticipation, passed on October 28, 1919. President Woodrow Wilson vetoed the law, but Congress overrode his veto with a second vote the same day.

The law authorized exemptions for religious, medical, and industrial purposes. Adults were permitted to make a limited amount of homemade, "non-intoxicating" wine and cider.

On the day prohibition became the law of the land, the Las Cruces newspaper was moved to opine:

> *[nothing]*

The event was not mentioned.

The El Paso Herald noted large, mournful celebrations of drinkers in New York, Chicago, and other U. S. cities. It also reported:

> *"As the end of the world for the 'wets' approaches, the transporting of liquor from El Paso into Juarez [Mexico] continues with a vengeance."*

> *"Thursday the heaviest shipments of liquor on the records of the custom house were taken across the bridge, and W. W. Carpenter, collector of customs for the port, estimated that since January 1, 741 barrels and 5567 cases of whisky had been exported... worth almost $3,000,000."* [1]

It was either get it out of the country or have it destroyed.

Theaters Continue to Change Hands

On January 1, 1920, R. W. Pierce sold the Star and Airdome theaters to Earl R. McMullen. Pierce had purchased the theaters from Cupp & Sons in November, 1919, who had in turn bought the property from Emil Brutinel three months earlier.[2] [3]

McMullen, no doubt recognizing that the recurring turnover in theater ownership was hurting business, renamed the Star the "A-muse-U" and issued a public statement:

> *"We announce the formal opening of the A-muse-U Theater, formerly the Star."*

> *"Having taken over THE STAR THEATRE just recently, I wish to announce my intentions. Las Cruces is one of the best towns in the valley – the people are*

just like the town, and I have figured it out they would enjoy and support the very best amusement that can be obtained. Heretofore they have not had shows of the class that I am getting in the A-muse-U."

"I have come to this town to make my home and to live. I'm going to do all one man can for a town in the public, and will greatly appreciate the cooperation of the public in this way. I am putting in the very best and will depend upon the public to enjoy my shows and give me my share of the patronage."

"The prices will be on a foundation instead of a pivot, and will not take wings, only when I have a show well worth every cent asked."

"Any time you're not pleased with a show I will greatly appreciate your coming to me and tell me so. If you like it, tell your friends so. I'm going to endeavor to please you. I'll give the best – the public must do the rest."

"Watch the 'A-muse-U' grow."

"Earl R. McMullen" [4]

In April, McMullen changed Airdome to Movieland and announced a new ticket pricing policy, eliminating the need for patrons to carry pennies:

"The present prices range from 10 cents to 35 cents with war tax added, causing the necessity of making change in pennies, but under the new schedule the flat prices will include the war tax." [5]

A few days later, the Movieland caught fire, but it was able to reopen quickly:

"The public didn't hardly believe it possible, but on Saturday afternoon bills were distributed announcing the regular program for that evening, which was given. Not only that, but in spite of the heavy loss, the proprietors have given and are giving benefit performances for the Salvation Army drive." [6]

A New Owner

In spite of his optimism, McMullen was unable to make the theaters pay, as he sells them in May, 1922, to Charles D. Stewart.

Stewart had previously owned several theaters in Colorado, and was an experienced manager. It was soon apparent that his move to Las Cruces was just the first step in an ambitious theater acquisition plan. [7]

Stewart immediately opened the Movieland and announced his policy for managing the two theaters:

"Summer is really here. The management of the Star Theatre have resumed the open-air theatre for the good weather."

"During the summer months there will be only one play, starting promptly at 8 o'clock. This is due to the fact that the screen is too light to start earlier, and the programs are too long to run through twice." [8]

In July, 1922, when a showing at the Movieland was rained out, Steward reminded his viewers of his policy:

"Mr. Stewart wishes to inform his patrons that whenever the weather is unfavorable his pictures will be shown indoors at the Star. Often there is no time to announce the change beforehand and considerable confusion and misunderstanding can be avoided by going directly to the Star in the event of rain or heavy winds." [9]

In August, 1922, Stewart decided the Star needed a new name:

"C. D. Stewart... is conducting a contest for the most popular name for his theatre. Movie fans may enter the competition by filling out and returning one of the cards now available at the box office." [10]

By the third week of September, Stewart had his new name, Navajo:

"This week the name of the 'Star' theatre was changed to 'Navajo.' With the change of name the management intends making a number of improvements to make it a better playhouse and one that will be more attractive to theatre goers." [11]

Six weeks later, the Las Cruces newspaper reported that Stewart was making his own films:

"A great deal of interest was taken in the operations of the moving picture camera man last week. Close-ups of several prominent Las Cruces people have been taken. The camera also took in a panorama of Main street, featuring the Catholic church and the Loretta Academy. Mr. Stewart has sent for $200 worth of raw film to be used in making the real features in which the cast will be local artists. He also hopes to take a great many scenes in the valley, all to have their first showing in the Navajo Theater, after which they will be released to other houses in the state and nation." [12]

Stewart began the 1923 year by scheduling an interesting promotional appearance. On January 20, Ruth Roland:

"...dashing, daring, queen of Pathe Serials, will introduce her new chapter to patrons of the Navajo Theater. The first episode is 'The Log Jam' in three reels. A thrill is introduced in the opening scene with Miss Roland, as the heroine Ruth Reading, being dragged from the path of a falling tree."

"The final thrill is tremendous, showing Ruth crashing down a steep and sharply winding track on a runaway freight car." [13]

THE LOG JAM was the first of the 15 episodes of THE TIMBER QUEEN. The film, made in 1922, is mostly lost (several episodes can be seen on Youtube.com.) Roland's film career stretched from 1908 to 1935. She almost always did her own stunts, no matter how dangerous.[14]

Two weeks later, the Navajo opened the blockbuster spectacular NERO, raising the ticket prices to 25 and 50 cents. The picture was filmed in Rome, with an Italian cast and thousands of extras:

"Nero is a wonderful story, well acted and sumptuously produced, and can be recommended to those who ordinarily care little for the movies." [15]

In May, 1923, Stewart changed the Movieland's name to Navajoland and announced its seasonal opening:

> *"The out door play house has been re-arranged for this season and every-*
> *thing possible has been done to give the patrons the maximum of comfort. Space*
> *is provided for those who wish to view the pictures from their cars."* [16]

> *"Cushions furnished gratis with reserved seats."* [17]

A few months after acquiring the Las Cruces theaters, Stewart bought the Gem Theater in Socorro, New Mexico and the Mojave Theater in Alpine, Texas.[18] By June, 1923, he had bought three more theaters: the Pastime Theater in San Marcial, New Mexico, the Star Theater in Fort Lupton, Colorado, and the Lux Theater in Littleton, Colorado.[19] A few months later he added the Central Theater, in Belen, New Mexico, to his chain.

Theaters Sold Again

In October, 1924, after running the Navajo and Navajoland Theaters for two years, Stewart sold them B. B. Hinman. No reasons are stated for the sale.[20] Hinman was an experience theater operator, having owned and managed the Strand Theater in Trinidad, Colorado, since 1918.

> *"Failing health, necessitating a change in climate, prompted Mr. Hinman*
> *to sell the Strand...."* [21]

As each new owner invariably did, Hinman renamed the Navajo, changing it back to Star.[22]

Five months later, in March, 1925, Hinman sold the Star and Navajoland to J. F. Laubach.[23] Perhaps this action by Hinman, like his purchase, was motivated by his poor health.

Laubach kept the Star name, but renamed the Navajoland back to Airdome. The Airdome's new tag line was: *"Go where they all go – the coolest place in the city."* [24]

Shock of Competition

In February, 1926, Laubach learned, probably with a shudder, that a large, modern, two-story movie theater was to be built on Main Street, not far from his Star Theater. The new theater duly opened five months later, thoroughly changing Las Cruces' theater landscape.[25]

Photos

1919 Movieland Theater flyers. Before and after being the Movieland, it was the (new) Airdome Theater. Courtesy Archives and Special Collections, New Mexico State University.

A-Muse-U Theater flyer for the 1919 film THE FALL OF BABYLON, directed by D. W. Griffith. Before being the A-Muse-U, it was the Star Theater. Courtesy Archives and Special Collections, New Mexico State University.

THE FALL OF BABYLON flyer, second page. Courtesy Archives and Special Collections, New Mexico State University.

A-Muse-U Theater flyer for the 1920 film THE TURNING POINT, directed by J. A. Barry. Courtesy Archives and Special Collections, New Mexico State University.

STAR THEATRE

"*Ten Commandments*"

DECEMBER 24, 25, 26

NIGHT ONLY

PLEASE EXCHANGE AT BOX OFFICE

PRICE 83c

Star Theatre ticket for the 1923 film TEN COMMANDMENTS. Courtesy Archives and Special Collections, New Mexico State University.

Chapter 6 | Coolest Place in the Valley – 1926-1929

On May 12, 1925, the partnership of Carroll T. Seale and Bert G. Dyne purchased the Hacker Hotel, located at 211 N. Main Street, from its owners for $10,000.[1] The run-down, 40-year old building on the site was demolished. In its place, Seale and Dyne built a state-of-the-art, two-story movie theater. The theater designer was El Paso architect Otto H. Thorman, who adopted an Italian Renaissance Revival style for the building.[2]

Prior to buying the site and building the theater, Seale and Dyne had struck a deal with the Central Theatres Corporation of Denver to operate the theater.

To determine the new theater's name, the operators chose the long-standing tactic of staging a contest. At the end of the contest, they announced the new name: Rio Grande Theater.

One of the contest entrants cried unfair:

"Editor of the Citizen:"

"Regardless of all sophistry and bunk as to the wording of that theater name contest, the word 'preferred' did not occur in the notice, but decidedly stated, that the word 'should not be one of over six letters.' No matter if the one who is alleged to have won it did get her list in earlier than the others who gave the name 'Grande,' the name Rio Grande was not entitled to consideration as it is a name of nine letters."

"The standard of this contest, as decided upon at Denver, is not only unjust, but dishonest..."

"To award a contest contrary to the public and published form is to award a premium for lawlessness and irregularity. What chance had the other 86 contestants?"

"Yours truly,"

"Edw. S. Doan" [3]

Rio Grande Theater Opens

On July 24, 1926, the Las Cruces newspaper announced the Rio Grande Theater would open in five days:

"A treat indeed is in store for those who have anxiously awaited the opening of this truly wonderful institution which is a great credit to the Southwest, the builders who have had the foresight to visualize the future in their enterprise and the operators for the confidence they have placed in the community in the manner they have equipped the theatre."

"Replacing the old style painted scenery, the stage is to be hung and decorated in a lavish manner with velvet drapes and curtains as is the auditorium

proper. The foyer and aisles are carpeted in a rich red and the lightning [sic] is as modern as has yet been installed in even the larger theatres in the cities."

"A washed air cooling system maintains any desired temperature with its clean pure air as distributed scientifically throughout the house, the mammoth organ will be operated by Miss Elsie Dean Bristol who comes direct from one of the corporation's Denver theatres, which assures all lovers of accurately played pictures a treat in store for them." [4]

The "washed air cooling system" was an evaporative air conditioner, the first in Las Cruces. To enhance the impact of the cooling system on patrons, every other vent on the wall of the theater was a painted vent, distinguishable from the real vents only through close inspection.

The theater opened officially on July 29, 1926. The movie selected for the opening was MARE NOSTRUM, directed by Rex Ingram. The *New York Times'* movie critic Mordaunt Hall had given the movie a mixed review. Even then, the movie critic's basic stance of an haute attitude and a pseudo-intellectual tone is evident. Some quotes from the review:

"The German submarine and the Wilhelmstrasse spy system during the World War are the theme of Rex Ingram's picturization of Blasco Ibanez's 'Mare Nostrum,' which was presented last night before an audience that appeared to be left slightly dazed by the weird delivery of the film. It is an effort that in the second half has its full quota of thrills, but in the end it reminds one of the Von Tirpitz edict—'Spurlos Versenkt!' The heroine and the hero have met their deaths and so have the villains; the comedian alone is left to drift back to his Spanish port aboard a flimsy raft."

"Mr. Ingram goes about the unfolding of this narrative with a dislike of haste. He seems to tell you that you must gaze upon his story as he tells it or not at all, and therefore it is not until just before the first half has come to a close that interest in the picture is really awakened; that happens to be through a scene in which a stout German Frau Doktor of the German Secret Service, her faithful and beautiful aid, Freya Talberg, and a Spanish skipper, drink a toast to the Emperor Josef."

"The first sequence dealing with the sinking of a British vessel by a submarine is graphically filmed. The Mediterranean is a tame stretch of blue to a wireless operator. He had just said 'Hello' to his colleague aboard the Californian. Then one perceives the submersible sneaking after its prey, and subsequently the Californian receives her death blow in an explosion of spray and fire. Aboard the other vessel all is tranquil; then the wireless operator gets the S. O. S., but gradually the sinking ship is covered by water. The commander of the submarine pushes his cap back over his shorn head and checks off the British steamship as having been sunk."

"Freya is arrested as a spy and taken from Marseilles to the St. Lazare prison, in Paris. In the course of usual motion picture events Freya would have been saved at the last minute. One awaits it in this film. She is taken to Vincennes in

the early morning, and the soldiers line up. The buglers sound 'Taps' after making a flourish with their brass instruments. Freya had made a petition to be shot in furs, feathers and expensive clothes; it was granted. She had walked proudly to the white stake against which she rests. Her hands had been tied with rope. An officer winces before the order is given to fire. When that order comes, the rifles blaze and nothing more is seen of Freya until a weird idea of nebulous figures under the sea is portrayed at the end of the picture."

"Aside from the effective photography in Spain, Italy and France and the dramatic sequences concerned with the submarine's deadly work and the shooting of a woman spy, this production does not do justice to the talent of the man who made 'The Four Horsemen of the Apocalypse' and 'Scaramouche.' His last production, 'The Arab,' was lovely but a slow story that did not boast of much in the way of drama." [5]

"Mare Nostrum" is Latin for "Our Sea." Beginning in Roman times it referred to the Mediterranean Sea. During World War I, it was common shorthand for the fight for control of the Mediterranean between the two warring sides. "Spurlos Versenkt" is German for "sunk without a trace." It refers in this context to the sinking on June 27, 1918, of the Canadian hospital ship *HMHS Llandovery Castle* by a German submarine. The phrase had been used in a secret telegram by the German ambassador to Argentina to describe German sea policy that had been intercepted and made public by British Intelligence. [6]

Probably no one in Las Cruces read the *New York Times'* review. The opening was a big success:

"W. L. Gullett, manager of the new Rio Grande Theater got off to a good start Thursday night when he opened this fine new playhouse because the house was packed and the play was up to expectations, and then some."

"It is needless to say that he will continue to have full houses as it is Mr. Gullett's intention to bring only the best plays." [7]

Prices for the showing were 40 cents for the main floor, 30 cents for the balcony, and 15 cents for children.

Laubach Struggles to Compete

In the winter months, prior to the opening of the Rio Grande Theater, Laubach ran large newspaper ads for his Star Theater. In May, two months before the Rio Grande opened, he closed the Star and opened the Airdome for its summer season, as usual. The tagline for the Airdome advertisements was *"cool, fresh, natural air."* [8]

After the opening of the Rio Grande, both theater operators ran weekly newspaper ads for their showings. The Rio Grande ads were always larger. The prices for the Airdome were 10, 25, and 40 cents. The prices for the Rio Grande were 15, 30, and 40 cents. Laubach dropped the cool, fresh, natural air tagline and the Rio Grande added the tagline *"coolest spot in the valley."* [9]

In October, 1926, Laubach closed the Airdome for the winter and opened the Star. The Rio Grande changed its ad tagline to *"comfortably heated, perfectly ventilated."* [10]

By early 1927, it was apparent that the competition with the Rio Grande was driving Laubach out of business. He had quit running ads every week. Then in May he closed his theaters and announced:

> *"Entire Change of Program"*

> *"Week Commencing Sunday May 22"* [11]

Laubach never resumed business. On July 23, 1927, the Las Cruces newspaper reported:

> *"Kohn and Fairchild Amusement Co., operators and owners of twenty-five theaters, mostly in Colorado, bought and took possession of the Rio Grande Theater on July 20 and of the Star Theater on July 21. The admission prices at the Rio Grande will remain the same, at the Star a definite policy will be announced next week."*

> *"W. L. Gullett will remain as manager of both houses...."* [12]

The following week, the new owner announced:

> *"...the prices at the Star will be reduced to ten and twenty cents and [it] will be open Saturday and Sundays so long as business justifies, starting July 31, tomorrow."*

> *"The cream of the picture market will be shown at the Rio Grande at the same price of admission as during competition [with the Star], with very few exceptions."* [13]

The next week, the owner reiterated this two-tier policy:

> *"...the cream of the market will be shown at the Rio Grande."*

> *"The Star will [show] principally the virile outdoor type of pictures so popular with a great many."* [14]

Rio Grande Gets a Wurlitzer Organ

On June 26, 1928, the top-tier status of the Rio Grande was enhanced by the installation of a Wurlitzer organ, replacing the piano that had provided music before:

> *"Joe Marriott, expert organ builder of the Wurlitzer Company, arrived Thursday morning and is working night and day to complete the work of installation which will all be accomplished in ample time to open Tuesday. Needless to say Las Cruces is getting something in the music line usually found only in the large cities and contrary to the usual custom, no outside organist will be imported to play the instrument, it being the policy of the K & F Amusement Co. to employ only local people where possible to do so...."*

> *"Anything that could be said about the expense or size or elaborateness of the instrument would only sound like flashy publicity and we are modest, but ask that you be the critic and let us know if you think Las Cruces is getting all it deserves in the amusement line."* [15]

Star Theater Burns Down

On March 3, 1929, the Star was destroyed by fire:

"One of the most devastating fires in the history of Las Cruces occurred this forenoon, when fire of unknown origin burned the interior and roof of the Star theatre building...."

"The fire had a great start before it was noticed, and but for the prompt and heroic work of the firemen who had to leave their work in different parts of town, the two story brick building belonging to Sam F. Bean, would also have been consumed." [16]

Fox Buys the Rio Grande Theater

On August 24, 1929, the theaters owned by the K & F Amusement Company, which included the Rio Grande, were bought by Fox West Coast Theaters, a theater ownership company started in 1921 by William Fox. The name of the Rio Grande was changed to the Fox Rio Grande.[17]

By the time he acquired the Rio Grande, Fox's theater corporation owned more than 1,100 movie theaters, making it, at the time, the largest theater chain in the country.[18]

In a full-page ad announcing the new ownership of the Rio Grande, Fox explained that October 14, 1929, was a special day for him:

"The silver jubilee of the William Fox Theatres."

"Tomorrow, October 14th, and continuing for the entire week, every Fox theatre throughout the United States will observe this event with a splendid entertainment befitting the attainment of a quarter century of remarkable growth." [19]

The ad also stated:

"The story of William Fox is the History of the Motion Picture – a pioneer, who, by his courage, integrity, independence and foresight has transformed an obscure enterprise into a magnificent art. It is significant that the Fox enterprise is the only Motion Picture endeavor to attain a quarter century of world-wide growth and success." [20]

This was not just hype. As noted in Chapter 1, Fox had opened his first moving picture venue on October 14, 1904, in New York City, as an Edison exhibitor. In 1911, he sued Edison's Motion Picture Patents Company, alleging it was a monopoly, as described in Chapter 1. Although he lost that lawsuit, his action led directly to a subsequent federal lawsuit that ruled the Patents Company an illegal monopoly.

With the end of the Patents Company, film production and distribution was open to all who wanted to get into the business. Fox quickly expanded into big-time film production by founding the Fox Film Corporation, his first film being A FOOL THERE WAS starring "sex vamp" Theda Bara, who portrays a femme fatale, perhaps the first in cinematic history. (*Life Magazine* wrote that the film *"probably exerted a more profound influence on contemporary thought than any picture that has ever been produced."* [21])

But there was more to Fox's silver jubilee:

*"**Far more important than even the entertainment, will be a message from William Fox of vital concern to the future welfare of every patron of Fox Theatres.** In 25 years the Fox Organization has grown from a nickelodeon to the most gigantic enterprise in the world. This unparalleled success could not have been possible without the whole-hearted response and liberal support extended to William Fox by the American people. **On this occasion William Fox will disclose through the Movietone screen of each Fox Theatre his plan to repay you in material profit for this quarter century of generous patronage.*"* [22] (Bold in original)

Time Magazine published the following response to Fox's jubilee:

"Last week came the Silver Jubilee (25 years) of the Fox Theatres, announced by lavish two-page newspaper advertisements that told of gala performances, mysteriously adding: 'Far more important than even the entertainment, will be a message from William Fox of vital concern to the future welfare of every patron of Fox theatres.'"

"In 500 of the 1,100 Fox theatres throughout the U. S. audiences heard this message delivered through Fox Movietone. The birthday gift was advice that Fox patrons buy outright as many shares as they could afford of Fox Theatres Corp. operating and holding company for his gigantic chain. As special inducement they were told of plans for future expansion and the large earnings that were possible."

"Expansions promised by Mr. Fox far outstripped the ordinary bounds of showmanship. He promised not only installation of his 'grandeur' proscenium-filling screen, and cinema houses devoted to newsreels, but magnificently he offered one fourth of his fortune (which newsmen were permitted to estimate at $36,000,000) to develop visual-oral instruction in schools. 'On the theory,' he said, 'that one picture is the equivalent of eight words' and that words uttered by college presidents are more potent than those of ordinary teachers, Mr. Fox visualized the time when 15,000,000 or 20,000,000 school children will have school hours reduced from six to three per day by listening to a talkie 'educator' instead of to a teacher....."

"Less convincing than his generosity was Cineman Fox's foxiness. Offered in 1925, Fox Theatres stock has paid no dividends, has never responded to continued reports of expansion. In 1928 its earnings were $1.91 a share. Previous attempts to distribute the stock, mostly held by speculators, have been unsuccessful. Early this year a group of brokers ran the stock to 37-7/8, but before much was distributed it broke to 21-1/2. Last week it was strong around 28 on belief that the Fox Birthday plan, if successful, will reduce the floating supply." [23]

Las Cruces Gets Talkies

On October 19, 1929, five days after Fox's silver jubilee, the newspaper announced the arrival of talkies:

"Sound Pictures Coming"

"A matter of great interest to Las Cruces theatre goers is that tomorrow the Fox Rio Grande Theatre, one block west of Church street, will open up their sound projector system which they have been busily installing for the past week or so. From the character of pictures with sound which have been booked for the coming weeks it is quite apparent that Las Cruces is to have just as high grade entertainment in that line as the largest cities in the country. Las Cruces is to be congratulated upon this fact and it is comforting to know that with this beautiful playhouse, and the installation of this most adequate and modern sound projecting system which is the product of Western Electric and the best made; together with the management afforded by the great Fox West Coast Theatre chain which now owns the Rio Grande, Las Cruces folks will not have to go to El Paso nor anywhere else to see and hear the best shows produced. It is also a matter of satisfaction to Las Cruces people that manager W. L. Gullett is to remain in charge of the management of the Rio Grande." [24]

First Talkie

Las Cruces' first talkie was shown Sunday, October 20, 1929. The film was THE FLYING FOOL, starring William Boyd. Boyd later became famous as "Hopalong Cassidy."

THE FLYING FOOL is the story of a WWI pilot with that nickname who falls in love with his brother's girlfriend. To settle who gets the girl, the brothers "fight it out" without guns in the air. After taking extraordinary risks, both brothers land safely and the girl decides she is in love with the "Flying Fool."

The schedule for the Fox Rio Grande's first week of talkies was:

Sunday-Monday, THE FLYING FOOL
Tuesday-Wednesday, GERALDINE
Thursday-Friday, THE SINGLE STANDARD
Saturday, DIAMOND MASTER [25]

Stock Market Crashes – October 24, 1929

The people who attended the Thursday showing of THE SINGLE STANDARD, starring Greta Garbo, probably enjoyed it. It is impossible to say how many people in Las Cruces heard of or worried about the stock market crash that day. Certainly no one knew that people would later consider that event that day – Black Thursday – the beginning of the Great Depression.

If Fox had not bought the Rio Grande when it did, Las Cruces would probably not have gotten sound for years. Within two years, movie revenue nationwide was down by 40 per cent and many thousands of theaters had been closed.[26]

Screen with a Voice

The sound picture revolution was a long time coming. As far back as peephole movies, Edison had tried to connect synchronized sound with movies by using record players. But it was almost impossible to keep the sound and pictures in sync. When a film broke and had to be spliced, for example, all synchronization was lost.

In 1926, Warner Brothers Pictures, Inc., using Western Electric technology, thought they had finally solved the sync problem with a system they named Vitaphone. In the Vitaphone system, the record player controlled the film projector. In addition, the Vitaphone system required the presence of a Vitaphone engineer constantly monitoring the sound/picture synchronization and manually adjusting that synchronization as necessary.[27]

On August 6, 1926, in New York, Warner Brothers publically exhibited a sound picture using the Vitaphone system for the first time. The film was DON JUAN, and the sound consisted of synchronized musical accompaniment, not dialog. Tickets cost ten dollars.

The New York press gave DON JUAN excellent reviews:

"The most gala of all gala movie premieres reopened the Warner Theater last night with the first public trial of the Vitaphone and Warner Brothers' presentation of John Barrymore in 'Don Juan.'"

"So realistic were the tonal effects that the audience clapped for encores after each number…. The Vitaphone synchronization took the place of the customary corps of musicians." [28]

The technology behind the Vitaphone was top secret:

"While the Vitaphone is thoroughly protected by patents… Warners permit nobody to see the delicate mechanism that produces in life-likeness a singing and musical screen. Nobody is permitted 'back stage.'"

"The purely technical aspects of Vitaphone and its principles and coordinating sound and action will ever remain a secret…."

"Meanwhile thousands… marvel at the 'screen with a voice.'" [29]

In spite of these dramatic claims of secrecy, Warner Brothers licensed the Vitaphone technology to other studios, enabling them to make sound pictures also.

But Vitaphone was not a satisfactory sound system. The process of making Vitaphone movies was complicated, labor intensive, error-prone, and expensive; and fitting theaters to display the films could cost $25,000 or more.[30]

On January 19, 1929, Fox Studios introduced Movietone, a system where the sound was recorded on the film along with the pictures.[31] Although the two systems co-existed for a while, Movietone's sound-on-film technology was vastly better than Vitaphone, and, with improvements over the years, became the sole method of making sound pictures, until the development of modern digital technology.

Photos

ANNOUNCING

THE OPENING OF THE

RIO GRANDE

THEATRE

(Operated by the Central Theatres Corp'n. of Denver)

THURSDAY, JULY 29th, 7:30, 9:30

Presenting

"MARE NOSTRUM"

REX INGRAM'S MASTERPIECE

A Powerful Story of the Sea

With

ALICE TERRY and ANTONIO MORENO

ADDED ATTRACTIONS

Pathe News	Aesop's Fables
Topics of the Day	Elsie Dean Bristol, Organist

PRICES

Main Floor	40c	Balcony	30c
Gallery	15c	Children	15c

Newspaper announcement of Rio Grande Theater opening, July 29, 1926. *Las Cruces Citizen*, July 24, 1926.

Newspaper announcement of William Fox Theaters' Silver Jubilee, October 14, 1929. *Las Cruces Citizen,* October 12, 1929.

Rio Grande Theater, circa 1928. Courtesy Archives and Special Collections, New Mexico State University.

Rio Grande Theater auditorium, showing the Wurlitzer organ installed on June 26, 1928. Undated photo. Courtesy Archives and Special Collections, New Mexico State University.

Chapter 7 | Depression Years – 1930-1939

As it became apparent in 1930 that the United States was entering a serious economic downturn, now known as the Great Depression, most observers were predicting the movie industry would be little affected. 1928 and 1929 had been the best years ever for the business, and there seemed to be few reasons to believe the momentum of those years would not continue. And, indeed, 1930 was another record movie year.[1]

But by 1931, the cumulative impact of the economic depression was slamming movie attendance. Overall unemployment in the country was 16 percent, and would reach 29 percent in 1932. Total gross business revenue for 1931 declined 28 percent. Wages for those lucky enough to still hold jobs declined 30 percent.[2]

U. S. movie theater attendance in 1931 dropped a punishing 12 percent. The industry publication *Variety* reported:

"...the decline was such that it leaves an open question whether the moving picture will ever again know the popularity of those peaks it reached in the silent era and then again with sound."

"Any perusal of figures for '31, and a minute or two of retrospect, will tab the approximate 25,000,000 people the theatres are estimated to have lost weekly...." [3]

In 1932, attendance declined another 15 percent.[4]

New Theater Opens – Del Rio

On February 22, 1930, a new theater opened:

"Last Saturday night witnessed the opening of the Del Rio Theatre, an independently owned and operated theatre in the location formerly occupied by the Elite Confectionery." [126 South Main Street]

"Mr. Able Davis, of Denver, is the sponsor of the project and is well pleased with the reception accorded his venture in Las Cruces, as packed houses at the opening performances, together with expressions of appreciation from representative theatre goers at having a high class theatre giving the best obtainable in silent pictures."

"Music is provided by non-synchronous amplification as especially designed for theatre purposes, and met with the instant approval of the many who have heard the instrument. Several hundred upholstered chairs provide comfort to the patron, together with good ventilation, pleasant surroundings and courtesy to be noted everywhere."

"One has but to visit the Del Rio to learn what can be accomplished by good taste and experience in so short a space of time, which has been consumed

in preparing for the opening. Green velour drapes in abundance, rich carpet throughout the entire foyer and aisles, soft toned lighting effects, and flowers in profusion, gave one the feeling of being entertained in a much larger theatre at higher admission prices."

"It will be the policy of the Del Rio to present four shows daily – 1 and 3 o'clock in the afternoon, and 7:15 and 9:15 in the evening – and the prices are to be always 10 cents and 25 cents." [5]

The policy of the new theater will be the best obtainable silent productions. [6]

That an experienced entrepreneur would stake so much capital on a non-custom-built, silent movie theater just four months after Fox had installed the equipment for exhibiting talkies shows that many in the industry did not yet appreciate the revolution that was sound pictures.

It is unclear what non-synchronous sound system Davis was using. Among the non-synchronous systems on the market in 1930 were: Orchestraphone, Magnola, Symphonium, Vict-o-phone, Vocafilm, and Bristolphone.[7]

In November, 1930, the Las Cruces newspaper reported:

"A new Neon electric sign is being erected at the Del Rio Theatre this week. The sign will be nine feet in height and will display three colors, blue, green and red. Mr. Davis expects to have the sign in operation Monday."[8]

Within two months, the Del Rio was out of business.

Las Cruces Gets BILLY THE KID World Premiere

On October 4, 1930, the Las Cruces newspaper announced the city would host the world premiere of BILLY THE KID:

"Billy has a rich part in the history of adventure in New Mexico, especially around here. It seems very fitting the show should make its first appearance in Las Cruces. But such a thing never happened before. New pictures that may properly be rated 'great' are usually assigned to Chicago, New York, or Los Angeles for their first appearances."

"But this time, it's Las Cruces."

"Places nearby, perhaps actually in Las Cruces, will be in the picture. Mesilla will be there in all its glory. Pat Garrett will be there, shooting with two guns at the same moment. The Kid's business activities were carried on largely in Lincoln county, and it was appropriate the picture should be filmed in Lincoln. Many scenes in and around that town will appear." [9]

BILLY THE KID was directed and produced by King Vidor. John Mack Brown played Billy and Wallace Beery played Garrett. It was released by Metro-Goldwyn-Mayer.

The three-day showing was an outstanding success:

"An unofficial estimate is that 4,000 people saw the picture of the play, Billy the Kid, at the Rio Grande theatre recently. Some local people paid their way in

to see the same show as many as four times. To enter twice was a common thing. The picture was shown twelve times...."

"Those who looked at it were entranced.... But many left the house in tears, for we knew it is a historical fact that this so charming Billy had but a few days of life left to him. The Drama does not account of that, but ends with the youth riding rapidly in the direction of Mexico, followed by a very darling girl."

"The monstrous crowds, and indescribable enthusiasm of those who saw the picture, certainly stamp it a winner. It is a world picture. Before many months it will be seen in London, Paris, Cairo, and other foreign cities." [10]

The article continued with something quite prescient:

"In time Billy the Kid will be to New Mexico what Robin Hood has ever been to England. A legendary creature of wonderful marksmanship, courage, courtesy, and generosity, Pat Garrett, sheriff of Lincoln county in the picture, will be our bravest peace-officer, and indeed was, perhaps, the only man who could have dealt successfully with conditions in his country then."

The movie was based on the 1926 book *"The Saga of Billy the Kid"* by Walter Noble Burns. Burns' book was the first book-length biography of Billy since Pat Garrett's 1882 *"The Authentic Life of Billy, the Kid, the Noted Desperado of the Southwest, Whose Deeds of Daring Have Made His Name a Terror in New Mexico, Arizona, and Northern Mexico."* The Burns book was a huge success (unlike Garrett's) and stimulated lasting interest in Billy, who had been mostly forgotten by the public.

In conjunction with the movie's premiere, the Las Cruces newspaper published several striking accounts of encounters by locals with Billy:

"We are indebted to Frank Islas, of Las Cruces, for a good story of the day Billy was brought to Las Cruces to appear before the District Court...." [11]

Following that luring introduction is a long account of Billy's actions in Las Cruces. But Billy was never brought to Las Cruces. He was taken to Mesilla, which was the county seat at that time, tried and convicted there, and then taken to Lincoln to be hanged. He was able to escape from Lincoln by killing his two guards just days before his scheduled hanging.

After its showing in Las Cruces, BILLY THE KID moved to the Silco Theater in Silver City. Following the Silver City showing, the movie was distributed nationwide.[12]

The reviews of the movie in the national press were good, praising the acting of both Brown and Beery, and noting the film's historical accuracy. In the publicity for the film, the studio noted:

"William S 'Bill' Hart lent to John Mack Brown Billy the Kid's own gun, taken from him by a man named Stewart, a member of the posse which captured him December 26, 1880. This gun is authenticated by affidavits from Jim East, another posse member who recently died in Douglas; Charlie Seringo, once foreman of the IXL ranch, and others." [13]

In spite of the testimonials, the gun was a fake, never having been owned by Billy. He was captured December 24, not December 26.

The historical accuracy of the movie was greatly over estimated, but it did accurately reflect what was presented in *"The Saga of Billy the Kid."* Burns based much of his book on oral accounts of Billy's life, and most of the factually inaccurate information in his book (and the movie) resulted from those oral accounts.

William Fox Forced Out

On April 7, 1930, newspapers headlines across the country announced that William Fox had been forced out of his companies.[14] The Associated Press put it this way:

> *"...a 60-hour conference preceded the withdrawal of William Fox from the head of the $300,000,000 motion picture industry and theater chain which he had watched grow from a $1,600 nickelodeon and was as dramatic as any scene ever filmed in the Fox studios."*

> *"When the session ended Fox no longer was one of the greatest figures in the industry but in his place rose Harley L. Clarke, of Chicago to assume control of the business...."* [15]

The United Press reported:

> *"William Fox, whose name is known in every country of the world as a titan of the amusement industry, surrendered his control today of the two huge organizations which he founded – the Fox Film corporation and the Fox Theaters corporation."*

> *"Climaxing a bitter financial struggle which dates back to the turbulent days of the October stock market collapse, Fox resigned as president of the film corporation and sold his controlling interest in the two companies to Harley L. Clark, Chicago utility magnate...."* [16]

The financial troubles that led to Fox's ouster were caused by his massive purchase of theaters in 1928 and 1929. To finance these purchases, Fox had borrowed heavily. Following the stock market crash in October, 1929, he fought desperately to keep his creditors from calling their loans by offering a bankruptcy re-organization plan. But his creditors saw that it was to their great benefit to insist on immediate and full repayment, knowing he could not comply, enabling them to buy his stock at great discount and take over the company.[17]

As part of the negotiations leading to Fox's resignation, he was promised that he would remain on an advisory board for five years, permitting him to retain some say in the running of the company. After the deal, the new owners denied they had made such a promise.[18]

On May 28, 1935, Fox Film Studios and Fox Theaters merged with the much smaller Twentieth Century Pictures, becoming Twentieth Century-Fox. The Fox businesses had lost money every year since Fox's forced exit. Twentieth Century, which had been founded a year earlier, had been making money and was the dominant merger partner.[19]

Surviving the Great Depression

As the depression increasingly bit into the ability and willingness of city residents to spend money, the management of the Rio Grande responded by turning the theater into a community center. Special events were organized where food donations for those needing food were accepted for tickets. Talent Nights were promoted, where those who wished could perform for the public before the showing of the evening movie. On various anniversaries and other important local events, free refreshments were offered to attendees. Raffles and contests were held, where prizes donated by merchants were given away to lucky ticket holders or winners.[20]

Whenever possible, promotions were tied to movie subjects. For example, when a movie dealing with doctors was shown, the wives of doctors were given free attendance. When a movie dealing with lawyers was shown, the wives of lawyers were given free attendance.[21]

Patrons were even permitted requests:

"The Fox Rio Grande theatre has inaugurated a request night program which will enable the public to see a re-showing of its favorite pictures in addition to the regular feature picture scheduled for that date. Cards are being distributed by the theatre management containing a list of favorites such as Bad Girl, Daddy Long Legs, Connecticut Yankee, Smiling Lieutenant, Dracula, Dixiana, Reducing, Tom Sawyer, and Whoopee. All a theatre patron has to do is place a check mark against the picture he enjoyed enough to care to see again." [22]

The Rio Grande facility was improved, expanding the screen.[23] The Epicurean comfort of the theater was touted:

"...old Sol can not get the best of you when you enter the front doors, where a cool and refreshing breeze meets you, and makes you feel that you are near the seaside or the mountains. The mammoth cooling system used by the Rio Grande washes and purifies the air every minute, which makes it 20 to 30 degrees cooler inside." [24]

On September 4, 1931, the larger of the two banks in town, the First National Bank of Las Cruces failed, after a panicky bank run sparked by a rumor. The bank president promised:

"'When the hysteria subsides, we will re-open the bank.... The bank is sound and we can pay 100 cents on the dollar when we re-open.'" [25]

When the bank did re-open on September 26, depositors were forced to agree to keep 25 percent of their deposit in the bank for a least a year. The remainder of their deposit could be withdrawn gradually over a series of months.[26]

New Movie Tax

On June 6, 1932, President Hoover signed the Revenue Act of 1932, a massive tax increase intended (unsuccessfully) to fight the depression. The act placed taxes on almost all consumer products, and greatly increased income taxes, raising the top tax rate from 25 percent to 63 percent.[27]

The tax allotted to movies, like the World War I movie tax, was tiered. There was no tax on tickets costing 40 cents or less. On tickets costing more than 40 cents, the tax was one penny per 10 cents. Thus, a 45 cent ticket cost 49 cents, a 50 cent ticket cost 55 cents, and a 60 cent ticket cost 66 cents.[28]

The additional cost to consumers of the movie tax in 1932 was 44 million dollars. To mitigate the effect of the tax, many theaters dropped ticket prices to 40 cents or less.[29]

In Las Cruces, the Rio Grande implemented a system of discount tickets. If you purchased anything at a Las Cruces merchant that was a member of the incentive program, you received a "community ticket" that entitled you to a 20-cent discount on an evening movie ticket, thus dropping the price below the taxable threshold.[30]

Rio Grande Theatre Burned

On July 28, 1933, the *"Rio Grande was badly damaged by fire.... The gallery was wrecked and the main floor was damaged by smoke and water."* [31] The fire broke out after the theater had closed following the last screening.

The initial assessment was that the fire was caused by defective wiring. That explanation was called into question when a series of intentionally set fires occurred over the next few days:

"Authorities today were investigating what is believed to have been an attempt to burn the Las Cruces courthouse."

"The building was filled with smoke when a janitor opened it at 4 a.m. Three old overcoats soaked in oil were smoldering in a ventilator under the public health office. The fire apparently had been started only a few minutes before."

"Authorities said there had been considerable agitation recently among unemployed for public work in Las Cruces."

"It is believed that someone attempted to burn the building to create work through construction of another."

"The Rio Grande theater was badly damaged by fire of undetermined origin last week. It will have to be rebuilt."

"Two other mysterious fires were extinguished with little damage last week in the residential section." [32]

Although it was thought initially that the theater building would have to be torn down and rebuilt, it proved possible to salvage much of the original structure.[33] If the theater had been burned to create jobs, the arsonist must have been disappointed with his work, as repairing the theater provided fewer jobs than new construction would have:

"...rapid progress is being made on the building which will probably be ready for use on November 7. The theatre is now being decorated, and an artistic job is being done by both California and local workmen.... There is an additional seating capacity of one hundred, making a total accommodation of 818." [34]

While the Rio Grande was out of commission, the Las Cruces public was not deprived of movies:

"...the sound equipment has been set up in the Del Rio theater, further down Main street, and Manager Sheedy opened the show last night and offers the public the same excellent programs as usual." [35]

The grand opening of the Rio Grande was November 7, as promised:

"The new Rio Grande theatre, which has been completely remodeled following the fire..., celebrated its opening night with an attendance of over one thousand local patrons...."

"Telegrams of good wishes were on display from such well known movie stars as Gary Cooper, Lillian Harvey, Janet Gaynor, Mae West, Frederic March and Warner Baxter."

"The feature picture on the program was 'The Footlight Parade....'" [36]

The new interior design continued the original Italian Renaissance Revival style:

"The Renaissance beauty of the 15th century has been carefully carried out on the ceilings, the foyer with its highly decorated gold panels and gorgeous polychrome, the walls of the lobby are plain putty color enriched with shaded gold and highly decorated cartouches."

"Six magnificent wall drapes will cover the side walls of the auditorium, while the main stage will have a new vocal-light screen and turquoise satin plush curtain decorated with hand painted motifs."

"The outer lobby with its beamed ceilings create a pleasing view as one enters, as does the main entrance with its Spanish rip-rap-tile floor and tile bordered box office."

"The old gold chandeliers will throw their soft glow on the Wilton carpets of Spanish designs and coloring which are being especially woven by Eastern mills." [37]

Following the re-opening of the Rio Grande, the Del Rio was closed again.

Del Rio Theater Burns

On December, 5, 1934, the worst fire to that date in Las Cruces' history burned *"an entire business block"* on Main Street. The fire started at 4 a.m. in the Pullman café:

"Before the firemen were able to get the blaze under control, it had spread from the cafe to the old Boston store...."

"The Kut Rate Grocery then caught fire and for a while the flames threatened to reach the Eric Hotel, and guests fled the building."

"It was not until after the fire had spread to an empty theater building, the Del Rio, that the blaze was stopped." [38]

The owners of the burned buildings announced that *"as soon as the ruins cool off so the place can be cleared... we plan to rebuild."* [39]

Del Rio Theater Re-Opens

Ten months after the fire that damaged it, the re-built Del Rio Theater was acquired by Fox Theaters, now a subsidiary of Twentieth Century-Fox:

> *"Henry Westerfield, manager of the Fox Rio Grande theatre announces the reopening of the Del Rio theatre on Saturday, November 2...."*

> *"'We have spent much money in reconditioning the Del Rio... and we plan to have the best shows at low prices.' The Del Rio will be open only Saturdays and Sundays...."* [40]

Once again, the theaters of Las Cruces were consolidated under a single ownership.

In March, 1938, the name of the Del Rio was changed to Teatro Del Rio and it began showing only Spanish-language films. This appears to be the first time a Spanish-language film was shown in Las Cruces, a belated recognition of the Spanish-speaking segment of the citizenry.[41]

The first film shown was MISTERIO DEL ROSTRO PALIDO (Mystery of the Ghastly Face), directed and produced by the pioneering Mexican filmmaker Juan Bustillo Oro.[42] The movie was a horror film featuring a mad scientist, who, in trying to cure a rare disease, became a Frankenstein-like figure.

Evidently the patronage was insufficient to support an all Spanish-language format, because a year later, the Teatro Del Rio management decided to remodel the theater and resume showing English-language films. The name was changed back to Del Rio and the ticket price was dropped to 15 cents for adults, 10 cents for children.

> *"The Del Rio Theatre, newly decorated, repainted and with a brand new cooling system installed will be opened next Sunday, April 9...."*

> *"The remodeling of the theatre and the installation of the modern cooling system represents the expenditure of a considerable sum...."* [43]

> *"One of the most important features of the new equipment is two large exhaust fans installed on the roof. These fans will remove all offensive orders that may be present...."* [44]

Following the upgrade, the Del Rio began using the tagline *"Always Cool."* [45]

Studio Anti-Trust Suit

On July 20, 1938, the U. S. Attorney General filed suit against the country's major film studios, charging the studios with "monopolizing the motion picture industry," because as film producers, they also owned theaters. This gave the studios control of a movie *"from selection of the story to final showing at the theater."* [46]

The eight studios named in suit were: Paramount Pictures, Inc., Metro-Goldwyn-Mayer (Loew's Inc.), Radio-Keith-Orpheum Corp. (RKO), Warner Brothers Pictures Inc., Twentieth Century-Fox Film Corp, Columbia Pictures Corp., Universal Corp., and United Artists Corp. Also named in the suit were 25 subsidiary corporations and 133 studio employees. [47]

The suit demanded that the studios *"divest themselves either of their ownership of theaters or of production and distribution facilities."* [48]

The defendants denied the charges. In June, 1940, they settled out of court with the government, making significant concessions, but not agreeing to divest their theater holdings. In 1945, the government reinstated its case against the studios, which it won in a trial in 1949. The studios were forced to sell their theaters, which remains the state of the law today.[49]

Photos

Flyer for BILLY THE KID, directed by King Vidor.

Rio Grande Theater world premiere of BILLY THE KID, opening day, October 12, 1930. Posed in front of the theater are the members of the State College marching band in military uniform, who gave a free public concert before the first showing. Behind them are numerous old timers who were special invited guests of the premiere, including several of Pat Garrett's children. Courtesy Archives and Special Collections, New Mexico State University.

Rio Grande Theater world premiere of BILLY THE KID, photo detail. Courtesy
Archives and Special Collections, New Mexico State University.

Del Rio Theater, circa 1932. Courtesy Archives and Special Collections, New Mexico State University.

Del Rio Theater, undated photo. Courtesy Archives and Special Collections, New Mexico State University.

Teatro Del Rio

LAS CRUCES, N. M.

MIERCOLES y JUEVES
6 y 7 de ABRIL

Dos Funciones Principiando a las 7 y 9 P.M.

ESTRENO DE LA CREACION CUMBRE DE LA
CINEMATOGRAFIA MEXICANA

LA PALOMA

El Alma de toda una raza en una Melodia Inmortal

MEDEA de NOVARA Con un Reparto de Estrellas

ARTURO de CORDOBA, Alfredo del Diestro, Alberto Marti,
Carlos Orellana, Sebastian Munoz, y Enrique Herrera

Un Gallardo Oficial Mexicano que deja su bandera y pone su espada al servicio de su corazon - Como un Mosquetero.

Un gran argumento para la primera gran Super-Produccion del Cine Mexicano. Con "LA PALOMA" se inicia el ciclo de las peliculas de altura.

Admission Adults 25c Children 10c

Teatro Del Rio flyer for the 1937 Spanish-language film, LA PALOMA, directed by
Miguel Contreras Torres. Medea de Novara played Carlota, Empress of Mexico.
La Paloma (the dove), composed in 1809, was said to be her favorite song. It was
also said that her husband, Maximilian, Emperor of Mexico, asked that the song
be played just before he was shot by a Mexican firing squad on June 19, 1867.
Courtesy Archives and Special Collections, New Mexico State University.

Mesilla and Mesilla Park

Mesilla

In 1910, two sets of entrepreneurs announced that they would soon open movie venues in Mesilla:

"Juan Verdugo and Pancho Bamis have purchased a moving picture machine and will have it in operation soon in the Estefana Bermudes Hall."

"Joseph Reynolds and A. J. Fountain [Jr.] will operate a moving picture show in Barilla [Barela] Hall." [1]

The stimulus for the movie venues, and the explanation as to why none had been proposed earlier, is that electricity had just been installed in Mesilla.[2]

The author has uncovered no evidence that Verdugo and Bamis successfully opened a moving picture theater. There is no further mention of their business in the newspaper, and they never applied for a business license.

Albert J. Fountain, Jr., no longer associated with Reynolds, opened his moving picture business in April, 1912, calling it *"The Fountain of Pleasure."* [3] [4] He had purchased the site for the theater for $125 on August 23, 1905, from trustees of the Home Mission Board of the Presbyterian Church, which had operated a church there since 1880.[5]

Local history says he built the theater in 1902, but that date is not possible.[6]

In 1890, Fountain had purchased the lot immediately south of the future theater site as a residence.[7] In 1912, when he obtained a license for his motion picture business, he let his license as a merchant expire, which he never renewed.[8] He was evidently using the theater site, which was next door to his residence, as a store, and he even continued the practice for a while as he listed his business in the 1912 Polk's Business Directory as *"Fountain of Pleasure Theatre, Curios and Art Goods."* [9]

Fountain operated his theater until April, 1916, when city license records note that he went *"out of business."* [10]

He resumed business in September, 1919, but lasted only until February 1, 1920, when he did not renew his motion picture license.[11]

The patchy nature of his movie business was undoubtedly due to the difficulty of competing with theaters in Las Cruces and their ability to get quality, first-run pictures. During the years that he ran his moving picture business, he also used the theater as a playhouse, staging live dramas and welcoming travelling vaudeville acts. To decorate the theater, he painted a series of murals on the walls, reflecting Mesilla history.

On June 1, 1927, Fountain sold the theater and his adjoining residence for $2,800 to Vicente D. Guerra.[12] In January, 1928, Guerra applied for a license for a moving picture theater using the business name Fountain Theater.[13] He ran the theater until April, 1931, when city records note he failed to renew his license.[14]

On opening the business, Guerra had installed *"sound equipment."* [15] Two facts suggest that what he installed was non-synchronous sound: (1) the high cost of synchronous sound and (2) his business failure just as synchronous sound became essential for survival as an exhibitor.

In 1938, Fountain re-purchased the theater after Guerra lost it in foreclosure. Fountain offered week-end, Spanish-language movies until 1951, when he closed the theater. The building was used for storage until 1963, when the Las Cruces Community Theater (LCCT), a volunteer group, was given permission by the Fountain family to use the theater for performances: [16]

> *"When LCCT members first surveyed the building they found 15 boxes of old chili, countless pinball machines, old record players and beer coolers."* [17]

Recognizing the need for additional space, in November, 1965, the LCCT purchased a 25 by 48 foot barracks from NMSU and moved it onto the vacant rear part of the theater lot. *"The ponderous move was made with only one fence being knocked down en route."* [18]

Modification of the barracks included:

> *"...installation of heating and lights [and] elaborate and well-equipped dressing and make-up rooms with banks of lights and mirrors. There is space now for costumes, set storage and a 'green room' for the cast's relaxation."* [19]

In 1974, the LCCT received $2,000 in grant funds for a *"new ceiling, raked audience seating, and restoration of murals inside and on the front of the theater."* [20]

The LCCT moved to the larger venue of the State Theater in Las Cruces in August, 1977, [21] and the Fountain resumed showing movies, taking the role of an "Art House." "Art Houses" in the 70s and 80s generally showed a mixture of risqué and foreign films. For example, the Fountain was the only venue in Las Cruces where MIDNIGHT COWBOY, THE DISCREET CHARM OF THE BOURGEOISIE, and LAST TANGO IN PARIS, all considered significant films today, were shown. [22] [23] [24]

The present occupant, the Mesilla Valley Film Society, began showing films at the Fountain Theater in 1989. [25]

Mesilla Park

On May 11, 1937, the Mission Theater was opened in the unincorporated community of Mesilla Park. (In 1970, a small portion of Mesilla Park was annexed by Mesilla. In 1976, the remainder of Mesilla Park was annexed by Las Cruces. [26] [27])

The builder and owner was Rod Bason, a Las Cruces businessman. The manager was Herschel Wheeler:

> *"The lovely building is of Indian pueblo style, and fits in beautifully with the colorful and historic period of the Southwest. That atmosphere is further enhanced by the ten sunken panels in the main auditorium, the work of Floyd Crews, El Paso artist, which depict Indian scenes."*

"The theater, with a seating capacity of 500, is air conditioned and acousti- cally treated. Among the many features is a lounge and stage, 15 feet deep and 25 feet wide...."

"The exterior of the building is white plaster, with window and door frames of blue. Woodwork, inside and out, is antique finish." [28]

The opening was a *"gala"* event attended by 2,000 people.

The initial tagline for the theater was *"Cool as an Igloo."* That changed to *"Your Home Town Show"* and *"An Independent Theater"* in later ads.

The ticket prices were 10 and 25 cents for evening performances, 10 and 15 for matinees. Tuesdays were *"pal night,"* when two could attend for 15 cents.

Saturday afternoons were *"kiddies' day,"* with events such as the Popeye Club:

"Popeye, as all know, loves children. In his every performance there's a fine moral. He's undoubtedly the most popular character in the comic world."

"It is only natural that Popeye would like to see a kiddies' club in operation here with Popeye, of course, as the shining star."

"The program every Saturday will feature a Popeye cartoon. The other part of the elaborate program varies each week. This week there will be two features and a serial." [29]

On March 5, 1938, the Mission Theater held what is probably the most bizarre event ever held in a moving picture theater:

"Mission Theatre To Give Away Live Baby"

"Does anyone want a real live baby girl?"

"Hershel Wheeler of the Mission theatre has announced that he will raffle a six weeks old baby girl at nine o'clock Saturday night. Patrons attending the theater Saturday night will be given tickets entitling them to a chance on the baby."

"Dr. Flannigan of Las Cruces will be present with a trained nurse to certify the baby's health, and a well known local attorney will be present to legalize the adoption papers. The parents and baby's name will be divulged to the winner and theatre patrons at that time."

"Mr. Wheeler said yesterday that 'If the winner does not want the baby, I shall be glad to have the adoption papers made out to me.'" [30]

The movies that night, suggestively, were OK DOCTOR and COURAGE OF THE WEST. The movie the next night was Frank Capra's appropriately anomalous LOST HORIZON.

The Las Cruces newspaper did not report any follow-up details about the baby raffle.

In August, 1938, Bason, evidently unable to compete with the Rio Grande, sold the Mission Theater to C. C. Dues, owner of the Crawford Theater in El Paso. Dues opened the theater only for Sunday showings.[31]

On January 28, 1939, K. M. Davis bought the Mission:

> *"Since Mr. Davis arrived and 'took over' the Mission Theatre last January 28, the business conditions of the Mission Theatre have grown from practically nothing to a business substantial and progressive."* [32]

In spite of his optimism, Davis only lasted another 30 days, after which he was forced to close.[33] Even permitting women to attend matinees for free could not salvage his business.[34]

In November, 1939, Fox Inter-Mountain Theaters announced they would take over the Mission:

> *"It will be completely remodeled and renovated, redecorated, and will have entirely new sound equipment and machinery...."*

> *"A fine program of spring shows is being booked."* [35]

Photos

Patrons lined up to enter the Fountain Theater, circa 1920. Courtesy Archives and Special Collections, New Mexico State University.

Fountain Theater, after a light rain, 2009.

Fountain Theater, showing mural painted by Albert J. Fountain, Jr., 2014.

Fountain Theater, mural detail, 2014.

Mission Theater, Mesilla Park, 1948. Courtesy IHSF.org.

Mission Theater, Mesilla Park, 1952. Courtesy IHSF.org.

Mission Theater, Mesilla Park, 1946. To publicize the showing of THE WHITE GORILLA, Mission theater owner J. A. Weiss (in suit) built a cage on a trailer and pulled it around town with an employee (unidentified) in the cage in a gorilla suit to advertise the movie. Courtesy IHSF.org.

Auditorium, Mission Theater, Mesilla Park, 1947. Wall niche paintings by El Paso artist Floyd Crews. Courtesy IHSF.org.

The Forties – 1940-1949

On February 2, 1940, Fox Inter-Mountain Theaters re-opened the Mission Theater:

> *"The building has been completely refurnished and brightened with new calsomine [kalsomine] and tinting. The very comfortable seats from the Rio Grande theatre were installed at the Mission when new seats were put in the Rio Grande a month ago. New carpets have been laid."*

> *"The sound equipment at the Mission has been completely changed, and a Western Electric apparatus installed."*

> *"The Simplex machinery which will be used in projection is an assurance of good pictures...."*

> *"The Theatre will seat 408 people and is thoroughly air-conditioned for both winter and summer."* [1]

This action consolidated all of the area movie businesses under a single ownership.

With no competition, Fox Theaters was able to coordinate the showing of movies to maximize attendance and profit. The Rio Grande was the premier movie show house, getting the "best" films as soon as they were released, and charging the highest prices. The Del Rio and Mission Theaters were second-run show houses, charging less and receiving lower-tier films and re-releases.

Las Cruces Gets a Second World Premiere

In March, 1941, the Las Cruces Chamber of Commerce began a campaign to obtain the world premiere of THE OUTLAW, a new Billy the Kid movie, for the Rio Grande Theater. The arguments for opening the premiere in Las Cruces were that Billy had been tried and convicted in this area, and that the premiere of the first Billy the Kid movie had been held in the Las Cruces.

The cities of Santa Fe, New Mexico and Denver, Colorado, were also fighting to obtain the premiere.[2]

Eleven years earlier, in 1930, Las Cruces and its leaders had been euphoric at having a Billy the Kid premiere in the city. Not true of everyone in 1941:

> *"It is very surprising to note that the local Chamber of Commerce is stirring itself to get the premiere of the film, 'The Outlaw,' a picture exploiting the horse-thief, cattle-rustler and murderer, Billy the Kid."*

> *"Undoubtedly a large number of these business men are parents, and yet they set out to have a picture shown for the benefit of their offspring glorifying an outlaw...."*

> *"What did Billy the Kid ever do for New Mexico, except give it a bad name? In his 21 years he admittedly murdered 21 men, 'not counting Mexicans and Indians.'"*

> *"This is the man the Chamber of Commerce want to honor in Las Cruces."*

> *"The Chamber of Commerce seems to have a keen disregard for the fitness of things as well as its children's morals. For Las Cruces was the home for many years of the greatest peace officer in New Mexico, Pat Garrett, the man who wiped out this menace. His home is here and his body rests here, after he sacrificed his life that Las Cruces might be a place where the present Chamber of Commerce might earn its living and raise its children in safety from such murderers as Billy the Kid."* [3]

The writer repeats what was widely-believed at the time, that Billy had killed 21 men, plus an unknown number of "Mexicans and Indians." That was false. Billy indisputably killed five men, as historians have long known, of which only the last two were cold-blooded murders, committed in the act of escaping from jail in Lincoln. It is unclear if he committed the murder for which he was tried and convicted, although he was present at the murder and under the law that was sufficient for conviction.[4] (It is impossible to get into the nuances of the Lincoln County War and Billy the Kid's life here – but it is certain that Billy was singled out for unfair legal treatment, while everyone else of any culpability in the Lincoln County War, including many murderers, escaped all legal consequences.)

On April 4, 1941, the managers of the Rio Grande and Del Rio theaters travelled to Denver, to meet with representatives of Fox Inter-Mountain Theaters, to argue the case for opening THE OUTLAW in Las Cruces.[5]

On May 23, Fox Inter-Mountain Theaters announced that Las Cruces would receive the world premiere of a Billy the Kid movie – but not THE OUTLAW!

Instead, the Rio Grande would get BILLY THE KID, a Metro-Goldwyn-Mayer film produced by Irving Asher, directed by David Miller, and starring Robert Taylor as Billy.[6]

THE OUTLAW, produced and directed by Howard Hughes, was objected to by the censors of the Motion Picture Producers Association, delaying its release for years. (The censors objected to Jane Russell's dress in the movie, which deeply exposed her ample cleavage.)

MGM's BILLY THE KID was notably less accurate historically than King Vidor's BILLY THE KID, shown in 1930. In MGM's version, for example, the sheriff opposing Billy is called Jim Sherwood, not Pat Garrett.

But as inaccurate as MGM's BILLY THE KID was, THE OUTLAW was pure absurdist fantasy. It introduces Doc Holliday into the story, and has him killed by Pat Garrett. But the made-up story element that has echoed since through the years is the ending in which Billy is NOT killed by Garrett. Instead, with the fortuitous collusion of Garrett, the body of someone else is buried in Billy's grave, enabling Billy to live on without any fear of further pursuit.

The ridiculous and dishonest portrait of Pat Garrett in THE OUTLAW provoked the children of Pat Garrett to legal action:

> *"Survivors of Sheriff Pat Garrett, who killed Billy the Kid, the notorious New Mexico outlaw, have filed suit for $250,000 alleging the film 'The Outlaw,' besmirched the character of the pioneer New Mexico peace officer."*

> *"Those bringing the action include Oscar L. Garrett of Houston, Jarvis P. Garrett, now in South America, and two daughters, Pauline Garrett of Dona Anna County, New Mexico, and Elizabeth Garrett, blind musician and poet of Roswell, New Mexico."*

> *"Defendant in the action is a Hughes Tool Company, whose head, Howard Hughes, produced the film...."*

> *"Breach of contract is alleged. The plaintiffs asserted the film violates the contract by the characterization of Garrett that 'cruelly and unjustifiably besmirched the memory of their father.'"*

> *"The character known as Pat Garrett in the film, it is contended, in no way depicts the true Pat Garrett, who is described as one of the men who finally brought law and order to the Western frontier."*

> *"The picture has been condemned by the clergy on moral grounds and its approval by the Motion Picture Producers Association has been revoked."* [7]

The author was unable to determine the outcome of this suit, but it is reasonable to assume the plaintiffs received some satisfaction, as they apparently had some prior accommodation with the producer and the portrayal so violated the facts.

BILLY THE KID Opens

The BILLY THE KID premiere opened with a midnight showing on Thursday, May 29, followed by a four-day run. The Las Cruces newspaper gave the movie a good review, complimenting Robert Taylor's performance, but expressing disappointment that the outdoor scenes had been filmed in Monument Valley, Arizona, not in New Mexico.[8]

To help promote the film, the mayor of Las Cruces proclaimed the week Billy the Kid days. The Chamber passed out auto bumper stickers and offered a prize for the best store window decorated with a Billy-the-Kid theme. The prize was won by the Lenox Jewelry Store, which, besides displaying an original arrest warrant for Billy, issued at Lincoln on February 2, 1880, showed:

> *"Indian relics, an old wallet, an ancient Indian shoe, an old-fashioned door bell, a key winding watch movement, and an Indian purse, sewed together with deer sinew."* [9]

Despite the city's marketing efforts, attendance at the premiere was disappointing. None of the newspapers in the surrounding cities mentioned the premiere.

The reason for the subdued reception was undoubtedly the ever more menacing wars in Europe and Asia. On September 1, 1939, Nazi Germany had invaded Poland. In response, Poland's allies, Great Britain and France, declared war on Germany.

At the time of the premiere, the European war had gone almost entirely in Germany's favor. Germany had conquered and occupied Poland, Denmark, Norway, Netherlands, and Belgium. On June 10, 1940, Italy joined Germany as an ally. Twelve days later, France surrendered to Germany, permitting occupation of France's northern half and turning the southern half of the country into a collaborationist regime aiding Germany's war efforts.

On September 27, 1940, Japan and Germany became formal allies. The two countries had been de-facto allies since Japan had invaded China in 1937.

While the negotiations for the premiere were going on, Germany attacked Crete, having already taken mainland Greece. On May 30, 1941, the first big day of the premiere, Las Cruces residents woke up to the huge, bold newspaper headline "**ALLIED TROOPS FLEE CRETE IN FISHING BOATS**," and the news that the allied troops who were unable to flee were surrendering.[10]

The sense of impending threat to the United States reflected in the news accounts in the months preceding the BILLY THE KID premiere contrasts starkly with the almost total absence of concern in the news accounts in the months leading up to the U. S. entering World War I.

New Theater Announced (State)

On June 20, 1941, Fox Inter-Mountain Theaters announced a new theater:

"It is to be located in the 300 block of North Main street... and is to cost, according to architect's estimates, between $15,000 and $18,000."

"Its dimensions will be 60 by 125 feet. It will have a seating capacity of 500. It's to be of Spanish architecture."

"Though exact admission prices haven't been fixed yet, it's to be a low-priced house... probably about half-way between admission charges of the Del Rio and the Rio Grande. It was designed to accommodate families who prefer a price-range between the two." [11]

Black Clouds Gather

On September 11, 1941, as part of its civil defense preparation, the State of New Mexico executed a blackout test:

"New Mexico today rallied its 530,000 residents for the nation's first test of a statewide blackout and civilian mobilization, set for tonight."

"The more than 70 communities participating will black out as big army bombers, simulating invader planes, roar over, beginning about 7:30 in the first areas 'raided.'"

"Approximately 13,000 will be actively engaged as raid wardens, special police, firemen, demolition and evacuation workers."

"In Las Cruces everything is in readiness for the blackout...." [12]

The Del Rio greeted the blackout test with:

"Be Safe During the Blackout Friday Night"

"Let the Del Rio Theatre be your 'Bombproof Shelter'"

"In the Midst of the Blackout – a blitzkrieg of laughs!"

"Joe E. Brown - Martha Raye in '$1000 a Touchdown' and Don 'Red' Barry in 'Texas Terrors'" [13]

New Mexico's blackout test was followed by blackout tests by other states.

War Declared

On December 7, 1941, Japan attacked U. S. ships and forces stationed at Pearl Harbor, Oahu, Hawaii. The devastating air attack was a complete surprise to U. S. forces.

The United States responded by declaring war on Japan:

"Exactly 33 minutes after President Franklin Delano Roosevelt informed an historic joint session of congress in the house chamber that the Empire of Japan had launched an 'unprovoked and dastardly' attack on the United States, declaring that a state of war existed between this country and Japan, congress had declared war on Nippon, scarcely 24 hours after Japanese planes opened their surprise attack on Hawaii."

"The war declaration, first by this government since the declaration against Germany, April 7, 1917, lacked unanimity by but one vote, as the senate voted 82 to nothing for the declaration, and 388 representatives voted yes, while Jeanette Rankin, isolationist Republican from Montana, repeated her 'no' vote of the last war, to be the lone dissenter...."

"Eight friendly nations had 'beat the United States to the draw' between the time, Sunday morning, of the Japanese attack on American possessions in the Pacific and noon today when the United States congress had formally declared war in retaliation."

"They are: Costa Rica, Paraguay, Nicaragua, Cuba, Haiti, Great Britain, Canada, and the Dutch East Indies." [14]

State Theatre Opened

On December 21, 1941, Fox Inter-Mountain Theaters announced that the grand opening of the company's new theater – the State Theatre – was to be Christmas Eve, December 24, 1941:

"Nothing has been overlooked to make the event one of the most brilliant ever staged here...."

"Gigantic Klieg lights, throwing hundreds of thousands of candle power, visible for 25 miles, will be set up outside the building and will sweep all quarters of the sky at three-minute intervals." [15] (A blackout test before the war – spotlights after war had begun!)

In a departure from tradition, there had been no public contest to select a name for the theater.

"When you attend the opening of the new State theatre... you'll have the 'sensation' of sitting in a building that is unique, not only in the state, but in

the nation, in that no more buildings of the same type will be constructed until after the war."

"There can't be, because all steel used in the steel reinforcing for walls and steel beams for the ceiling is under control of the priorities board and no new buildings using steel can even be started." [16]

The interior of the building:

"...is furnished in a light yellow, with blue wainscoting, and deep apricot velour drapes."

"The seats are all leather covered, and padded, designed for the comfort of patrons."

"The ventilating system will supply a change of air every two-and-a-half minutes for every person in the building...."

"The State will be staffed with at least eleven persons, including two new usherettes, Misses Betty Jo and Jane Rose Miller, twin sisters." [17]

The theater designer was El Paso architect Guy L. Frazer of the firm Frazer and Benner.

On opening night, the gala celebration began with a concert by the Las Cruces High School Band. That was followed by a brief speech by city officials and the reading of telegrams of congratulations from numerous actors, including W. C. Fields, Robert Stack, Rita Hayworth, Cary Grant, Betty Grable, Cesar Romero, John Wayne, and Don Ameche. The two features shown were VIVA MEXICO and TOP SERGEANT MILLIGAN.[18] [19]

With the opening of the State, Las Cruces had four theaters *"with a total seating capacity of approximately 2,500"* – all under Fox Inter-Mountain Theatres ownership.[20]

Del Rio Theater Upgraded

In January, 1942, the Del Rio became an all Spanish-language theater.[21]

On April 14, an attempt was made to burn the Del Rio down. This followed a series of larcenist fires, believed to be started by juveniles. In response the city imposed a curfew:

"'The fire siren,' Chief Roberson said today, 'will sound one blast at 8 o'clock each night for the duration of the present emergency and all juveniles under the age of 18 will be required to go home at that time.'" [22]

In May, Fox Inter-Mountain Theatres announced that the Del Rio would cease being exclusively Spanish-language and would be upgraded, placing it:

"...on par with any of its size in the state. A new, wide-vision screen will be installed.... Las Cruces definitely needs a middle-priced theatre, showing high class pictures...." [23]

Smoking in Theaters Banned

Provoked by a horrific fire caused by cigarette smoking in a Boston nightclub that killed 449 people and burned many more, the mayor of Las Cruces requested the city council to address the danger of smoking in local theaters:

"The existing ordinance... only forbids smoking in theatre projection rooms, where films would be exposed to fire; the new one will forbid smoking anywhere in a theatre and make it so binding that theatre operators will have to enforce it or be closed down." [24]

The ordinance duly passed December 2, 1942.[25]

THIS IS THE ARMY

On August 12, 1943, Irving Berlin's THIS IS THE ARMY premiered in Washington, D. C. A week later, the movie opened across the county.

THIS IS THE ARMY was based on the Berlin musical of the same name that had opened on Broadway on July 4, 1942.

From its conception, Berlin's goal was that all proceeds from his creation go to benefit men and women serving in the U. S. armed forces.[26]

Fox Inter-Mountain Theaters announced the movie would "premiere" at the Rio Grande in Las Cruces on October 21, 1943:

"All profits from the gala premiere showing of Irving Berlin's 'This Is The Army...' will be donated to Army Emergency Relief...."

"The picture, which was produced by Warner Bros as their donation to the relief fund, has been triumphantly received throughout the country...."

"[It] features a troupe of over 350 talented khaki-clad thespians, as well as Hollywood favorites as George Murphy, Capt. Ronald Reagan, Joan Leslie and Charles Butterworth."

"Army Emergency Relief has been organized by the army to give prompt financial help and other short-term assistance to all soldiers and their dependents who deserve help, whenever and wherever such help is needed." [27]

The showing raised $700 for the relief fund, a disappointment, as the theater was only *"partially filled."* [28] The probable cause was the ticket prices, which were $5.50 for the floor and $3.50 for the balcony. (Calling the showing a "premiere" enabled the theater to justify the higher than usual ticket prices.)

Nationally, the film raised over $9,500,000 and the Broadway musical over $2,000,000 for the Army Emergency Relief. This was the movie industry's single largest financial contribution to the U. S. war effort.[29]

Competition Returns

After remodeling the Mission Theater 1939, Fox Inter-Mountain Theaters kept it open for only eleven months – probably because of the company's plans to build and open the State Theater.

In August, 1944, after standing vacant for three years, the Mission acquired a new owner:

"The Allen family, long active in the theatrical management of New Mexico motion picture houses, are preparing to re-open the Mesilla Park theatre."

"Remodeling of the building is in progress now, and it will open soon, showing Paramount and other first-run pictures."

"S. E. Allen, at Lordsburg and Hatch, has been in the business 17 years; his son James will manage the Mesilla Park theatre." [30]

The Allen Mission Theater opened on October 12, 1944, facing seemingly crushing competition from Fox Inter-Mountain Theaters: the Rio Grande, State, and Del Rio Theaters.[31]

And it was – by December 1, fifty days later, the Mission was closed again.[32]

Germany and Japan Surrender

On May 7, 1945, Germany surrendered unconditionally to the Allied Powers, exempting the Soviet Union, to which it surrendered on May 9. The Allied victory was celebrated in Las Cruces with a parade of 3,000 school children and a Pioneer Park ceremony in which over 4,000 attended.[33]

On September 2, 1945, Japan formally surrendered. That event, too, was greeted by a city-wide celebration, although the tone was more somber, as the nation's newspapers were full of accounts of how atrociously Allied war prisoners had been treated by their Japanese captors.[34]

Mission Theater Turns Over Again

The Mission Theater stood vacant after its abandonment by Allen Theatres until July 5, 1946, when it was bought by J. B. McMahon. He ran the theater until March 14, 1947, when he sold the theater to J. A. Weiss and his son J. A. Weiss, Jr.

"They came here from California, although they have operated theaters in the Oklahoma City area for many years. The elder Weiss has had 25 years experience in theatre management, much of it in the Los Angeles area; while his son has been in the theatre business for 12 years."

"'We are very happy to have secured a theater such as the Mission with which to enter the business in New Mexico,' Mr. Weiss said today. 'We are proud of the Mission and enthusiastic over its potentialities.'"

"He said the Mission would fit proudly among the Los Angeles theaters of the better quality, and was enthusiastic over the murals in wall panels in the theater's auditorium. 'They were painted by an artist,' he said, declaring they would be covered with a florescent lacquer and would be illuminated by ultra-violet light...."

"Improvements in the theater's appearance and conveniences, including a well-lighted and patrolled parking area, were promised, and the interior will 'have an adequate air conditioning system, giving fresh air, hot or cold, depending on the season, to add to our patron's comfort,' Weiss added." [35]

The Weiss's adopted the tagline *"The Place of Comfort"* for their theater.

In October, 1948, the Weiss's held the first foreign-language "festival" in Las Cruces. The program, to consist of three foreign films, shown a week apart, required that patrons subscribe to the series in advance. The first showing was a Swedish film with English subtitles:

"Torment... is the first of the outstanding foreign movies to be shown at the Mission theatre here...."

"The central figures are a sadistic teacher in a boy's school, a sensitive student and a young shop girl with whom both men become involved."

"The picture is distinguished by majestic photographic effects and delicate direction and the startling theme is said to have been handled with rare frankness and artistry." [36]

The second film was the French-made PASSIONNELLE, based on a story by Émile Zola. The third was never identified in the newspaper, but was probably the French film ANTOINE AND ANTOINETTE, starring Roger Pigaut and Claire Maffei.

"First" Drive-In Theater

On June 25, 1948, the El Paso Amusement Company announced it would build a drive-in theater in Las Cruces: [37]

"Las Cruces will have its third theater and first of the drive-in type when the new Organ Drive-in theater on El Paseo opens its gates...." [38]

Although touted as Las Cruces' first drive-in, it was not. As noted in Chapter 3, the Airdome Theater, which opened July 11, 1914, could accommodate ten cars and 450 seated patrons.

On April 13, 1915, a second drive-in theater opened in Las Cruces – the Theatre de Guadalupe (immediately renamed the De Luxe Theater). The Theatre de Guadalupe had spaces for 40 cars and 700 seated patrons (Chapter 4).

So the Organ Drive-In should be considered the city's third.

The Organ opened August 19, 1948. It cost $6,000 to build and had space for 600 cars:

"The new theater boasts the most modern projection and sound equipment available. The sound system, a recent development for the benefit of drive-in theaters, allows patrons to hear just as well with the car windows rolled up as when they are down. This will make for more comfortable theater-going when the weather is cold or wet."

"A complete refreshment stand is located within the theater and an attendant will take refreshment orders from the car." [39]

The sound was supplied by open-air loud speakers at the base of the screen. This led to multiple city council complaints that the broadcast sound was a public nuisance.[40] In response, the owners installed a new sound system:

"The most modern thing in drive-in theater equipment was added this week to the Organ Drive-In Theater.... The addition of individual car speakers will make the entertainment offered by the theater even more enjoyable to its many patrons."

"These speakers... were installed at an expenditure of approximate $15,000."

"Another feature, volume control, makes it possible for the individual customer to adjust the outcome to suit his own need." [41]

Shortly after their installation:

"Six car-type speakers, valued at $35 each, were stolen from the Organ Drive-In Theatre Monday...."

"The speakers and one post were removed sometime during the show Monday night. The Theatre has offered a $50 reward for apprehension of the thief." [42]

The ticket price was 50 cents for adults; children under 12 were free.

Fox Remodels Theaters

On September 16, 1949, Fox Inter-Mountain Theaters initiated a remodeling program:

"Approximately $100,000 is or will be spent in the remodeling of the three Las Cruces theatres it has been announced here by Henry Westerfield, manager of the local theatres for the Fox Inter-Mountain Theatres."

"Work on two of the theatres, the State and the old Del Rio, which has been renamed the Plaza, is rapidly being completed. Plans have been completed for the re-opening of the Plaza, Tuesday, Sept. 20."

"It is also planned to remodel the Rio Grande theatre, the largest of the three, as soon as the Plaza is opened and in operation...."

"[The] State theatre will show first run pictures with three complete changes of program per week. The theatre has been completely remodeled with new front, new seating and completely redecorated. A large new sign has been erected."

"The Plaza theatre has been completely remodeled. New seating has been installed, new sound and projection equipment has been placed in the projector booth, new front put in place and a new sign and a new marquee provided. The Plaza is to show second run pictures as well as the best in Spanish pictures." [43]

Photos

Promotional drawing for State Theater opening, December 24, 1941. Courtesy
Archives and Special Collections, New Mexico State University.

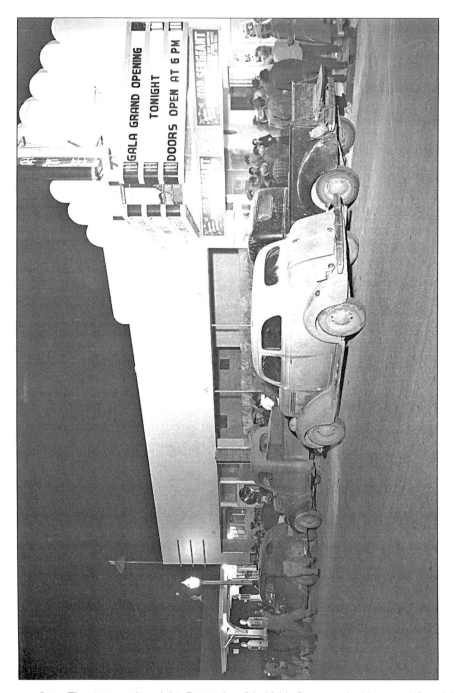

State Theater opening night, December 24, 1941. Courtesy Archives and Special Collections, New Mexico State University.

State Theater concession stand, undated photo. Unidentified employee. Courtesy Archives and Special Collections, New Mexico State University.

RIO GRANDE
MOVIE NEWS

LAS CRUCES, N. M.   DECEMBER 18, 1941

Happiness Keynote For Holiday
Movie Programs At Rio Grande

"Lady Be Good" Has Host Of Stars In Cast

A talent-filled cast, good direction, and a gay screen play studded with some of the most delightful singing and dancing seen on the screen in some time, combine to make "LADY Be GOOD," which will be seen this Friday and Saturday, a musical treat which patrons will want to see not once but twice.

The producers gave gone "all out" in it's array of talent for this picture which stars Eleanor Powell, Ann Sothern and Robert Young, with Lionel Barrymore, John Carrol, Red Skelton and Virginia O'Brien adding topnotch talent in featured supporting roles.

Miss Powell's dancing numbers are outstanding for their novelty and include a number in which a trained dog acts as her dancing partner. Also a highlight is the appearance of Miss Sothern in a singing role for the first time un-

NEW PROGRAM "CHANGE DAYS" AT RIO GRANDE

Starting this coming week, the Rio Grande will hereafter present it's Bargain Days on Tuesday and Wednesday instead of Wednesday and Thursday.

The week-end program will be presented three days, starting on Thursdays, and the Sunday program is shortened to two days only.

In this way, the Rio Grande will be enabled to present bigger and better attractions at all times.

Go To Movies Cure For War Jitters

In these days of war, the motion picture theatres of the country are offering perhaps the only sure escape from care and worry.

More than ever before, all of us have a need "to get away from ourselves," forget the war, our troubles, and enjoy ourselves for a few hours.

The Rio Grande theatre is establishing a policy of "nothing but entertainment," by eliminating all war references on the screen except those which are vital to the public interest.

LET'S GO TO A MOVIE!

der her M-G-M contract. Among her songs is the popular "The Last Time I Saw Paris," in which she is superb.

"YOU'LL NEVER GET RICH" GAY MUSICAL COMEDY OPENS SUNDAY WITH HAYWORTH STARRING

With a program reading like a tour of New York's White Way, picture titles such as "Lady Be Good," "You'll Never Get Rich," "Honolulu Lu," "Nothing But The Truth," and the Southwest's first showing of "Kathleen" which stars the new, grown-up Shirley Temple, this week at the Rio Grande theatre spells "H A P P I N E S S" to Las Cruces Movie-goers.

Fred Astaire and Rita Hayworth are the stars of "You'll Never Get Rich," a gay military musical which opens Sunday with the mystery story "The Night of January 16th" starring Robert Preston and Ellen Drew.

"Lady Be Good," termed M-G-M's biggest musical in years, is the Friday-Saturday attraction this week. Boasting a big cast which includes Eleanor Powell, Robert Young, Ann Sothern, radio's Red Skelton, Lionel Barrymore, and a host of others.

Bargain Days next week changes to Tuesday and Wednesday with Edward Arnold and Laraine Day appearing in "Unholy Partners" with "Honolulu Lu," co-starring Leo Carrillo and Lupe Velez.

The Christmas Day superprogram co-stars Bob Hope and Paulette Goddard in "Nothing But The Truth," with the new Shirley Temple in her first picture in two years, "Kathleen." The latter picture will be seen by Cruces fans before any town in the Southwest.

Rio Grande Theater Movie News, December 18, 1941, page 1. War Jitters: *"The Rio Grande theater is establishing a policy of 'nothing but entertainment,' by eliminating all war references on the screen except those which are vital to the public interest."* Courtesy Archives and Special Collections, New Mexico State University.

RIO GRANDE PROGRAM

FRIDAY and SATURDAY, Dec. 19 — 20

The Show World's Greatest
Song and Dance Extravaganza!

"Lady Be Good"

ELEANOR POWELL · ANN SOTHERN · ROBERT YOUNG

with LIONEL BARRYMORE
John Carroll · Red Skelton
Virginia O'Brien
M-G-M HIT

PLUS! The Three Mesquiteers   "UNDER TEXAS
Corrigan—Steele—Davis   in   STARS"

Note
New Opening
Days of
Programs!

SUNDAY—MONDAY Only — Dec. 21 and 22 only

FRED ASTAIRE
RITA HAYWORTH

ENTRANCING DANCING!
EXCITING BEAUTY'
All in the most
spectacular of army
extravaganzes!

"LET'S GO TO A
MOVIE!" — Now
—more than ever
you NEED the en_
tertainment and es-
cape you get at the
theatre! Forget the
war for a few
hours!

Robert
PRESTON
Ellen
DREW
JOHN HUBBARD
ROBERT BENCHLEY
with

Songs by
COLE PORTER

THE Night of
JANUARY 16th

YOU'LL NEVER GET RICH

Tues. & Wed., Dec. 23 & 24

Bargain Prices
Adults
30c Inc.
Tax

Edward G.
ROBINSON

UNHOLY PARTNERS

with
Edward ARNOLD

Honolulu Lu!

See "A CHRIST-
MAS CAROL" FREE by attending
the 8:30 Show — No charge.

Chrismas Day and Fri. & Sat.

PLUS
The FIRST
Showing
in the
Southwest
of

BOB HOPE · PAULETTE GODDARD
in

Nothing But The Truth

The New Shirley Temple in
"KATHLEEN"

With LARAINE DAY and
HERBERT MARSHALL

Rio Grande Theater Movie News, December 18, 1941, page 2. Courtesy Archives
and Special Collections, New Mexico State University.

RIO GRANDE MOVIE NEWS   **PAGE THREE**

A LINE ON HOLLYWOOD

HOLLYWOOD, Calif. —ELEA. NOR POWELL breaking three blood vessels in her hand, after rehearsing her new lightning tap dance, the "Hawonga," seen in "I'll Take Manila." . . . HEDY LAMARR wearing pig-tails for the first time in her life for scenes in "Tortilla Flat." , JOAN CRAWFORD building an outdoor gymnasium in her home for her adopted son, Christopher . . . BUD ABBOTT mourning the loss of his ten_year.old fox ter- rier pal, "Bitsy." . . . JUDY GAR- LAND selling an original to a national magazine . . . MYRA LOY preparing for her New York vacation . . . Deadpan singer VIRGINIA O'BRIEN proving that she has Hollywood's longest nails, on the "I'll Take Manila set . . . they are over a half an inch long TOMMY DORSEY planning to introduce MICKEY ROONEY'S new tune, "My Best Gal," when he opens at Hollywood's Palla. dium . . . gag.orginator RED SKELTON wiring his ice-box with a police siren to guard a. gainst houseguests "raiding the icebox." . . . title of best.dressed pooch going to ANN RUTHER- FORD'S French poodle, Henry . . he has an outfit for every occas. ion, including raincoat and paja. mas . . . autograph hunters hav- ing the time of their lives, when nearly every star on the M.G.M roster stopped on their way to work to watch MICKEY ROO- NEY doing opening scenes of lo- cation for "The Courtship of An. dy Hardy." . . . JOHN GAR- FIELD showing the cast of "Tor. tilla Flat" how to tie various knots . . he is an expert . . . ANN AYARS originating a new Spring color trend in "Out of the Past" . . . she wears a combination gray evening gown with silver acces. sories . . . BERT LAHR prepar- ing to move into his first Califor. nia home upon completion of his role in "I'll Take Manila." . . . LANA TURNER admitting her greatest thrill while on her New York vacation was viewing the city from the top deck of a Fifth Avenue Bus . . . . ROBERT YOUNG and his wife on their way back to Hollywood after at- tending the Boston premier of "H. M. Pulham, Esq."

Ann Sothern — Eleanor Powell — "Red" Skelton — John Caroll — Robt. Young Make "Lady Be Good" — Terrific!

"LADY BE GOOD" is the title of the picture from which the above star-packed scene was taken. Opening Friday "LADY BE GOOD" is a sure cure—for the blues.

"A Christmas Carol" Brought Back For Christmas Eve Show

The filmization of Charles Dicken's "A CHRISTMAS CAR. OL" which has become a film classic, is being brought back to Las Cruces for a Christmas Eve showing.

No film in the history of mo- tion pictures has succeeded in presenting the Christmas spirit like "A Christmas Carol." The story of Scrooge, which has thril. led millions will make YOUR Christmas a memorable event.

Shown as a FREE Owl Show, Bargain Day patrons may attend the Rio Grande Wednesday eve. ning and see this attraction in ad- dition to the regular show, at no extra charge.

Bargain Days Change To Tues. and Wed. With "Unholy Partners" and "Honolulu Lu"

Introducing a slight change in policy of Bargain Days, the first Tuesday_Wednesday program will present an outstanding bill which includes Edward Arnold and Laraine Day in "Unholy Partners," and Honolulu Lu" with Leo Carrillo and Lupe Ve- lez.

"Unholy Partners," is laid in the colorful prohibition era of returning World War heroes, transatlantic flights and marath. on dances, telling the story of two men, one a newspaper edi. tor, the other a racketeer. Bitter enemies, unique circumstances place them in joint control of a tabloid newspaper.

A hectic Hawaiian hullabaloo, "Honolulu Lu" presents the love- ly Latin Lupe Velez in a dual role. First appearing as a temper. mental, altogether charming member of a distinguished Span. ish family, with an uncle whose suave sophistication "fronts" for an innate inability to be honest.

Rio Grande Theater Movie News, December 18, 1941, page 3. Courtesy Archives and Special Collections, New Mexico State University.

BOB HOPE COMEDY "NOTHING BUT THE TRUTH" AND SHIRLEY TEMPLE'S "KATHLEEN" MAKE CHRISTMAS MERRY FOR CRUCENS

A MERRY, HILARIOUS CHRISTMAS is assured for Las Cruces with the showing of "NO. THING BUT THE TRUTH" star-ring the above comedians, Bob Hope and Paulette Goddard with Edward Arnold and Willie Best. Miss Shirley Temple in "KATH-LEEN" will be seen on the same program in which this new pic-ture enjoys the first showing in the Southwest.

New Show Is Radio Comedian's Best

"Kathleen" Showing One Of Southwest's First"

The signal's up once again for choice, laugh-loaded comedy, for another Bob Hope-Paulette God-dard picture is about to breeze in-to Las Cruces.

"NOTHING BUT THE TRUTH" coming to Cruces to make Christmas a merry event, fea-tures in it's exceptionally good cast Edward Arnold, Leif Erick-son, Helen Vinson and dancer Willie Best.

Fresh from his solid smash suc-cess in "Caught in the Draft," Hope this time will be seen as a stockbroker who bets $10,000 that he can tell the truth for 24 hours. With Paulette Goddard to add to the comedy and romance, the prospect of Hope having to tell the truth under all circumstances has all the earmarks of hilarious comedy. Knowing Hope as we all do by now, he's the one who can make the most of a situation as cleverly contrived as this. His position as a comedian in Holly-wood these days is second to none.

As the second half of the Christmas Super-program which runs through Saturday, the Rio Grande presents the first south-western showing of the new Shir-ley Temple picture, "KATH-LEEN." Her first film in two years, "Kathleen" brings a new, grownup Shirley to the screen in a different type role which will readily renew the affection of her millions of fans.

Her two years absence from the film studios has not diminished the charm, vigor and sympathe-tic acting qualities which made little Miss Temple one of the screen's outstanding personalities and one of it's leading boxoffice attractions. To be sure, the fam-ous blonde curls have given place to chestnut brown hair and the years have added an inch or so to her height, but it is the same sparkling, ingratiating Shirley who makes her appearance in the title role of "Kathleen," and it is a delight to have her back.

Free Defense Bonds For Bargain Day Patrons

A new plan will be presented Bargain Day patrons of the Rio Grande theatre next Tuesday and Wednesday when they will be permitted to enter their names on a guest register which will automatically make them eligi-ble to win a FREE Defense Bond at the theatre.

To make ownership of the De-fense Bonds, which is the same as "money in the bank," possible for a greater number of Las Cru-ces people, the Rio Grande plans to present at least two of the $25 bonds weekly to regular pat-rons.

No extra admission charge or other concession will be requir-ed by the theatre.

Major Studio Sneak Prevue Feature Of New Year's Eve Show

NEW YEAR'S EVE is the date, and 8:15 P. M. the time for the biggest frolic ever seen in Las Cruces, to be presented at the Rio Grande Theatre.

One regular admission charge will be made for a full night's entertainment which will include the regular program, added short subjects, vaudeville, intermissions and a "Sneak Prevue" of a Major studio production.

New Year's Eve will be usher-ed in with community singing, noisemakers and fun. Plan now to attend!

Rio Grande Theater Movie News, December 18, 1941, page 4. Courtesy Archives and Special Collections, New Mexico State University.

Rio Grande Theater showing 1946 film THE BEST YEARS OF OUR LIVES,
directed by William Wyler. The story is about the difficulties three World War II
veterans face adjusting to civilian life after the war. Courtesy Archives and Special
Collections, New Mexico State University.

Rio Grande Theater. The film won Academy Awards for Best Picture, Best Director, Best Actor, Best Supporting Actor, Best Film Editing, Best Adapted Screenplay, and Best Original Score. Courtesy Archives and Special Collections, New Mexico State University.

Rio Grande Theater showing 1948 film SEALED VERDICT, directed by Lewis Allen. The story is about a high-ranking Nazi being tried for war crimes who is able to prove mitigating circumstances. Courtesy Archives and Special Collections, New Mexico State University.

Chapter 10 | Fifties and Beyond

The Fifties began with the new theater format of the drive-in with in-car speakers versus the phalanx of the remodeled Fox Inter-Mountain Theaters – Rio Grande, State, and Plaza – versus the independently operated Mission Theater.

That was a lot of movie "seats" to fill every night.

As 1949 ended, movie publications reflected the industry's concern about revenue. 1947 had been the all-time peak year for movie revenue. It had declined every year afterwards, with 1950 expected to be worse than 1949.[1]

For indoor theater chains like Fox Inter-Mountain Theaters, the auto drive-in was a serious financial threat, as most of the early operators were independents. The drive-in format offered patrons what was essentially a private viewing box, which had many attractions: you could take the entire family, including babies in diapers; you could take your own food and drink; you did not have to dress up; you could smoke in your car; and grandma could even go to sleep in the backseat if she wanted to.

Young couples quickly figured out another delightful advantage: you could make-out while watching (or not watching) the movie.

There were disadvantages too, of course. Often the movie would start a little too early, before it was dark enough to see the screen well. Or it would start late, resulting in patrons honking their horns and shining their headlights in communal frustration. The sound quality could be poor or overlaid with radio interference. Mosquitoes could be a nasty problem.

Richard Milton Holingshead, Jr., who held a patent for the drive-in theater format (as noted in Chapter 2), was claiming that any who adopted the format owed his company royalties. Most operators ignored his claims, which led to various lawsuits in which Holingshead attempted to force compliance. One of these cases reached the U. S. Supreme Court in June, 1951, which denied Holingshead's legal right to collect royalties.[2]

Korean War

1950 <u>was</u> a bad year for the movie business.

On June 25, 1950, North Korea invaded South Korea. The news report of the North Korean action in the U. S. press contained no recognition that another "world" war was beginning.

> *"Communist invaders from North Korea threw a tank column to the outskirts of Seoul early today, and President Syngman Rhee blamed the crisis on 'too little and too late' American aid."* [3]

The South Koreans had no tanks and no weapons effective against tanks. Their army was outnumbered two to one, and poorly trained. It was a slaughter.[4]

On June 27, the United Nations Security Council passed a resolution recommending that all member states provide military assistance to South Korea. The Soviet Union was boycotting the Security Council, so was not present to veto the resolution (a monumental mistake).

On June 30, President Truman gave permission for U. S. troops to be sent to defend South Korea. The first of those troops arrived the next day. Ultimately, the United States would provide 90 percent of the non-Korean troops fighting for South Korea, and would pay almost all the costs of the war.[5]

As the Korean War approached the end of the third year of fighting, with the battle-front mired in an attritive stalemate that favored the North Koreans, morale and the economy in the United States were at low ebb. The Las Cruces newspaper reflected:

"America didn't start the Korean War. She has suffered more than 100,000 casualties in that war and paid a tremendous sum for a war that is no nearer over today than it was when it started." [6]

The Korean War tacitly ended July 27, 1953, when South and North Korea signed a truce. No peace treaty was ever signed.

New Drive-In Theater

In May, 1952, Hugh Cane, owner of a chain of drive-in theaters, announced that the drive-in theater he was building on Highway 70, on the eastern edge of Las Cruces, was nearly complete. The new theater, to be called the Rocket Drive-In, would have spaces to accommodate 500 cars. The viewing screen would be 68 by 43 feet in size:

"On the rear of the screen, facing the highway, a Neon light rocket with simulated fire emitting from the tail will be used as advertising for the theater. Two exits will speed traffic out of the theater area between shows." [7]

On July 21, 1952, the Rocket Drive-In opened to a capacity crowd, including people seated *"on nearby hillsides."* [8] The opening film was TOO YOUNG TO KISS, with June Allyson and Van Johnson. The opening ad noted:

"Our Projection Room is completely equipped with RCA sound equipment and operated by International Alliance of Theatrical Stage Employees and Moving Picture Machine Operators of the United States and Canada." [9]

The competing film at the Organ Drive-In was SANTA FE, with Randolph Scott.

Plaza Theater Closed by Fire

On December 8, 1952, a fire slightly damaged the Plaza Theater:

"The fire, which broke out in the kitchen of the De Luxe cafe about 8:15 a.m., swept through the second story of the building and engulfed the Las Cruces Hotel, then spread to the Del Rio bar next door to the cafe." [10]

The fire took four hours and 500,000 gallons of water to extinguish. Damage was estimated at $100,000. [11]

A Decade of Competition

The competition between the six theaters – Rio Grande, State, Plaza, Mission, Organ, and Rocket – continued to be intense throughout the 1950s. The theater ads for Friday showings sometimes filled a quarter or more of a newspaper page. During these years, the Plaza showed almost exclusively Spanish-language films.

One way drive-ins competed was by providing a playground for kids beneath the movie screen. This typically consisted of a merry-go-round, a slide, and a swing set, which could be used while waiting for the movie to start. In September, 1953, the Rocket upped its appeal with a new attraction:

> *"The Rocket Drive-In is happy to announce the installation of its new Miniature Train. This is a miniature of the General Motors Diesel Electric, with air brakes and all. It is the only one of its kind in the Southwest or Rocky Mountain District. So come out tonight and bring the kiddies for a ride. For grown-ups too."* [12]

On April 14, 1954, the manager of the Rio Grande announced the installation of the industry's newest screen and sound technology:

> *"....cinemascope is a completely engineered system for the practical presentation of wide screen pictures combined with true stereophonic sound and so designed to provide the greatest approach to realism in motion picture story telling yet achieved."*

> *"'This realism is possible because the cinemascope scheme permits using lenses during the photography which gives the most natural perspective.'"*

> *"...the cinemascope picture will be twice as wide as the old screen with a 2.55 ratio. In other words, what is seen on the screen will be about two and one-half times as wide as it is high."*

> *"The new screen... is 34 feet six inches wide, with a height of 14 feet eight inches."*

> *"The old system of producing sound... consisted of one speaker to the rear of the screen. With stereophonic, 10 speakers are used."* [13]

This upgrade ensured the Rio Grande remained the foremost movie theater in Las Cruces.

Theft and vandalism appeared to increase during these years. On September 25, 1952, the Rocket Drive-In was robbed:

> *"Witnesses of the robbery reported the bandit first drove up behind the box office, but was frightened away by an approaching car."* [14]

He returned a short time later and confronted the owner with a 45-caliber pistol. He was given $180, the receipts of the cash box. The cashier recorded the license number of his car as he fled, enabling the sheriff to track him down and arrest him the following day. In an irony probably not appreciated by the robber, the cashier of the Rocket was the daughter of the sheriff.

In July, 1954, the manager of the Rocket reported being "plagued" with the theft of speakers:

> *"He had lost between 180 and 190 speakers in the last several months, each costing about $16."*

> *"To cope with the problem... [he] had hired three young men to act as spotters for folks with sticky fingers."* [15]

A few days later, employees at the Rio Grande caught and turned over to the police two "students" slashing seats using a razor blade.[16]

In September, 1954, the Rocket marquee was "destroyed," prompting the theater's manager to post a $100 reward for information *"leading to the arrest and conviction of the person or persons responsible."* [17] The perpetrator was never identified.

Organ Drive-In Theater Renamed Fiesta

On January 16, 1955, the Organ Drive-In re-opened as the Fiesta Drive-In. The theater had been closed for several weeks to enable the screen to be enlarged and the projecting system improved. The opening shows were FOREVER FEMALE *("Fang and claw, two women fight for one man... in the jungle called Broadway!")* and WAR PATH.[18]

The Organ had apparently been losing business to the Rocket due to its aged condition.

Mission Theater Falters and Fails

On September 23, 1960, the Mission acquired new owners as a result of the death of the prior owner. The new owner, operating as Fairmont Enterprises, Inc., renamed the theater the Park Theater. The theater was only opened for weekend showings.[19]

Evidently unable to survive in business, Fairmont Enterprises, Inc. closed the Park following a last showing on March 18, 1962.[20] On April 24, 1962, the Park was offered for sale.

> *"Park Theater building in Mesilla Park, suitable for theatre, fully equipped; or other commercial uses. Priced at half of construction cost."* [21]

Rio Grande Theater Remodeled

On May 17, 1961, the Rio Grande re-opened following extensive remodeling:

> *"The entire front of the building has been given a new face.... The large electric sign on the front of the building has been completely rebuilt...."* [22]

The lobby was enlarged and equipped with larger concession stand.

> *"The most striking changes have been made in the theatre auditorium. The walls have been done over in a dramatic bitterroot orange color with a steel blue acoustical tile ceiling. Vast new stage draperies in the same bitterroot orange dominate the stage end of the room."*

"The new 40-foot screen has mother-of-pearl incorporated into its permanent plastic surface to give it the opalescent sheen."

"Forty tons of new refrigeration air conditioning equipment have been installed.... A completely new heating plant has been installed and the old unsightly steam radiators have been removed."

"The most striking change in the interior is the remodeled new balcony which was completely reconstructed in order to provide the upmost in seating comfort and the best picture viewing sight lines." [23]

The projection and sound systems were upgraded to the newest industry standards.

Adult Movies Arrive

On December 8, 1961, a Fiesta newspaper ad, for the first time, had the bold headline: **"Adult Entertainment."** Two movies were offered: GARDEN OF EDEN and THE BRIDE IS MUCH TOO BEAUTIFUL. The ad for the first film noted that it was ADULTS ONLY and had been *"Photographed at a REAL NUDIST PARK."* The second film, better known as HER BRIDAL NIGHT, starred Brigitte Bardot. [24]

The Fiesta had been showing somewhat risqué (by contemporary standards) films for some time. For example, a month earlier it had shown ADAM AND EVE and NUDE IN A WHITE CAR. (Clearly the Nude was a "good guy," or the title would have been NUDE IN A BLACK CAR.)

Aggie Drive-In Theater

On May 4, 1966, Lamar Gwaltney announced that the nearly completed construction at the intersection of the Truck Bypass and W. Hadley Street was a theater, to be called the Aggie Drive-In:

"The new outdoor theater will be open seven day a week with complete family entertainment and will have a snack bar. It will be equipped with Ballantyne Electronic Company double-cone speakers for better listening...." [25]

Note the stress on "family entertainment."

The Aggie Drive-In could accommodate 600 cars and was equipped with *"a giant single screen, measuring 90 feet wide by 60 feet high."*

"Gwaltney is presently engaged in the liquor business.... This is his first venture into the theater business." [26]

The double feature shown on opening night was CHARADE, starring Cary Grant and Audrey Hepburn, and I'D RATHER BE RICH, starring Sandra Dee and Andy Williams.[27]

In April, 1982, a second screen was added to the Aggie Drive-In and the theater was renamed the Aggie Twin.[28]

HANG 'EM HIGH

On May 25, 1967, the Las Cruces newspaper announced:

"There is going to be a real old-fashioned lynching on the Rio Grande – and what's more – local law enforcement officials will get an advance warning as to the time and place, but it will do them no good this time." [29]

The lynching was pretend. It was to be enacted as the opening scene of HANG 'EM HIGH, a new Clint Eastwood movie to be shot in the Las Cruces area. Leonard Freeman, the co-producer with Eastwood's production company Malpaso, had been in the area for several days, and had already *"found the ideal spot right on the river about 12 miles north of Las Cruces."* The lynch scene would come *"even before the 'Credits.'"* [30]

The lynching is the driving event of the movie. Eastwood plays ex-lawman Jed Cooper. He is herding cattle that he has just purchased back to his ranch when he is brutally arrested by a self-appointed citizen's posse. Unknown to the posse, the person who sold the cattle to Cooper had killed the true owners just prior to selling them to Cooper.

Cooper is hung by the posse and left for dead. A passing lawman comes upon Cooper hanging from the tree, and on cutting him down, is able to revive him. The remainder of the movie consists of Cooper ruthlessly pursuing the men responsible for his hanging and enacting suitable revenge.

The budget for the movie was two million, *"give or take a few hundred thousand dollars."* [31] Eastwood's fee was $400,000 plus 25% of the box office. [32]

On June 12, the pre-production team of Director Ted Post, Assistant Director Richard Bennett, Associate Producer Robert Stambler, Cameraman Leonard South, Wrangler Kenney Lee, and publicity man Art Wilde joined Freeman in Las Cruces. [33]

Formal shooting of the film began June 21. [34] The hanging scene was filmed June 29. [35] Eastwood did the entire scene himself, except for the swinging by his neck, which was done by his double Walter Scott. To build publicity for the film, 15 invited national and foreign press representatives were present at the lynching enactment. [36] [37]

The Las Cruces location shooting wrapped July 1. [38] The cast and crew then moved to California for additional shooting at MGM Studios. [39]

Evidently to protect his privacy, the newspaper never reported on any of Eastwood's non-movie activities, including when he arrived and left the area. The newspaper did carry articles on other actors and crew members interacting with locals. During the whole time the production company was in town, the Fiesta Drive-In showed Eastwood's FOR A FEW DOLLARS MORE.

The tree where Eastwood was hung is no longer standing and the river bank is now overgrown with thick brush.

Plaza Theater Converted to Stores

On November 9, 1969, the Plaza exhibited its last film. The theater was a casualty of the Urban Renewal plan adopted by Las Cruces in 1968. Urban Renewal was a massive social engineering project promoted by the Federal Government to rebuild urban areas in cities and towns across the United States. The Federal Government offered funds and guaranteed loans to buy property in suitably-defined "distressed" areas, enabling social "renewal" through remodeling and new construction.[40]

Las Cruces' decision to gut its existing downtown to take advantage of this program was the worst mistake the city has ever made. This decision is the reason that Las Cruces, unlike many southwestern cities, does not have a historic downtown.

The Plaza was the first downtown building to be "renewed." The cost was $22,000. The renovated building was occupied by a credit bureau, a title company, and a jewelry store.[41] [42]

Drive-In Consolidation

In June, 1964, the Fiesta was expanded by adding a second screen.[43] Second drive-in screens, and in some cases, three or four screens, were an innovation that swept the industry in the early sixties.

At the end of November, 1965, the Rocket closed. The last showing, on November 28, was a four-feature blow-out: THE HORRIBLE DR. HICHCOCK, THE AWFUL DR. ORLOF, HERCULE'S CAPTIVE WOMAN, and CREATURE OF THE JUNGLE.[44]

On January 26, 1967, the two-screen Fiesta was purchased by Video Independent Theaters, Inc., a national theater chain with more than 150 theaters. On February 20, 1967, the firm purchased the Aggie Drive-In, giving it ownership of both drive-in theaters in Las Cruces.[45]

On May 24, 1971, the Fiesta No. 2 screen was replaced with new, $35,000 screen.

"The new screen was necessary because of lighting from new businesses near the theatre on El Paseo Drive." [46]

"The new screen is all metal, closer to the projection booth, and set at a different angle." [47]

The new screen replaced the original Organ screen. The remodeling left Fiesta No. 2 with space for 458 cars and Fiesta No. 1 with space for 583 cars.

In June, 1978, the Fiesta became a one-screen theater again. In February, 1981, it closed.

Video-Twin Theater

On March 10, 1972, Video Independent Theaters, Inc. opened the Video Twin Theater:

> *"...many of the larger old theaters in the country are converting to two screens so that two different pictures may be shown simultaneously. The Video Twin concept, however, which is being put into practice in Las Cruces is a new one."*

> *"There are only two other theaters like the one in Las Cruces in the country.... Both of the others are in Oklahoma."*

> *"In each of the wings of the Video-Twin is a separate screen on which a feature-length film can be shown."*

> *"...no 'X' rated movies will be shown...."*

> *"The theaters themselves each have a seating capacity of 350. The seats have been spaced far apart and with wider aisles for maximum comfort...."* [48]

The opening of the Video-Twin had originally been set for January 26, 1972. But on January 24, just two days before the planned opening, the lobby of the theater caught fire:

> *"The concession counter area was completely destroyed by the fire."*

> *"Extensive smoke damage was also reported...."* [49]

The quick response of the fire department prevented the theater's twin auditoriums from catching fire.

The Video Twin was built on land backing the Fiesta Drive-In. The theater designer was Bill Waters of the architectural firm Lane and Waters. In 1978, Video Independent Theaters, Inc. announced that the two-screen Video Twin would soon become the four-screen Video Four, with the land for the theater expansion to be obtained by removing one of the two screens of the next-door Fiesta Drive-In.[50]

> *"A special new attraction in the new auditoriums will be a 'low-level' projection booth, with windows allowing patrons to watch the completely mechanized operation at work."* [51]

The initial plan for the dismantled Fiesta screen was to move it to the Aggie Drive-In, making that theater a two-screen drive-in. The screen was removed for the Video Twin expansion in December, 1978, but it was never reassembled at the Aggie Drive-In.[52]

On June 29, 1979, the Video Four had its grand opening, showing *"the greatest group of hits ever to run in Las Cruces at one time."* The opening movies were: ROCKY II, MOONRAKER, THE APPLE DUMPLING GANG RIDES AGAIN, and ESCAPE FROM ALCATRAZ.[52]

Allen Theaters Arrive

The Allen family and moving pictures have been inseparable since 1912. Although sources credit Frank B. Allen, the family progenitor, with opening the first moving picture theater in the state in Farmington, New Mexico, in that year, readers of this book know it was not the first.[53]

When Frank died in 1931, his son Russell Paul Allen continued the family business, expanding their theater holdings into other cities. In 1963, Russell's sons Larry and Lane, with then partner Boyd Scott, operating as Allen Theaters, began a huge expansion of the business within and outside New Mexico.

In June, 1982, Allen Theaters purchased all the working theaters in Las Cruces, a total of 11 screens: Rio Grande, Aggie Twin Drive-In, Video Four, and Cinema 4.[54] (The Cinema 4, a four-screen-theater, had opened February 26, 1982.[55])

On May 23, 1998, Allen Theaters expanded their Las Cruces holdings by opening Telshor Cinemas, a 12 screen theater.[56] In 2009, Allen Theaters added Cineport 10, ten screens with stadium seating and digital projection.

Rio Grande Theater Closes

On May 22, 1998, the Rio Grande exhibited U. S. MARSHALS, starring Tommy Lee Jones, Wesley Snipes, and Robert Downey, Jr. The people attending the showing that Friday evening knew it was the theater's last; it had been announced as such all week on the marquee.[57] (See photo.)

The following day, the new Telshor Cinemas opened.[58] Las Cruces movie patrons welcomed the opening of the comfortable, stylish Telshor Cinemas, with its state-of-the-art projection and digital sound. But the feeling of loss in the city at the closing of the Rio Grande was palpable, as was the determination that this distinguished, historic Las Cruces institution must be saved.

Doña Ana Arts Council Acquires Rio Grande Theater

Within months, Doña Ana Arts Council (DAAC) began working toward acquiring the Rio Grande Theater building. The intention was to create a premium exhibition space for events, movies, and performances in Las Cruces.

The effort got a huge boost when Jan Clute and Carolyn Muggenburg, granddaughters of Carroll T. Seale, one of the original builders of the Rio Grande, offered to gift their fifty percent ownership of the building to DAAC if the organization could raise the money to purchase the other half of the building and to restore it to its original Italian Renaissance Revival appearance.

It took seven years, but on September 16, 2005, DAAC celebrated its acquisition of the theater with a grand gala.[59]

This was a fit use for a grand Las Cruces institution. It saw silent films replaced by talkies. It endured intense competition by rivals. It survived the Great Depression, World War II, and the Korean War. It hosted two Billy the Kid World Premieres. It saw drive-in theaters spring up and die. And for almost 70 years, for just a little pocket change, for people of all ages, it provided the *"Coolest Place in the Valley."*

The End

Photos

Plaza Theater fire, December 8, 1952. (The Del Rio was renamed the Plaza in 1949.) Courtesy Dan Aranda.

Plaza Theater fire, December 8, 1952. Courtesy Dan Aranda.

Plaza Theater, 1957. Courtesy Archives and Special Collections, New Mexico State University.

Rocket Drive-In, 1952. Courtesy Estella Wilhelm.

1955 aerial photo of Rocket Drive-In. The site is bound on the west by N. Main St., on the south by E. Madrid Ave., and the east by N. Mesquite St. Courtesy Doña Ana County Community Development Department.

Rocket Drive-In, 1957. Courtesy Archives and Special Collections, New Mexico State University.

State Theater showing 1960 film THE SECRET OF THE PURPLE REEF, directed by William Witney. Courtesy Archives and Special Collections, New Mexico State University.

Rio Grande Theater showing 1962 film THE LONGEST DAY. The photo shows the horizontal marquee that was installed in place of the vertical marquee when the Rio Grande was remodelled in May, 1961. State Theater visible on far right. Courtesy Archives and Special Collections, New Mexico State University.

Rio Grande Theater concession stand following remodelling in May, 1961. Courtesy Archives and Special Collections, New Mexico State University.

Shooting HANG 'EM HIGH, White Sands National Monument, June, 1967. Director Ted Post on left, cameraman Leonard South on right. Eastwood mounting horse. Courtesy IHSF.org.

HANG 'EM HIGH, White Sands National Monument, June, 1967. Eastwood has just been knocked off his horse. Courtesy IHSF.org.

Eastwood, HANG 'EM HIGH, Cox Ranch, June, 1967. Courtesy IHSF.org.

Hanging scene, HANG 'EM HIGH, Rio Grande River, 12 miles north of Las Cruces, June 29, 1967. *Las Cruces Sun News*, July 2, 1967.

Hanging scene, HANG 'EM HIGH, June 29, 1967. The mountains in the background are the Doña Ana Mountains. The river is the Rio Grande River. Courtesy IHSF.org.

Eastwood's double, Walter Scott, hanging from tree, June 29, 1967. *Las Cruces Sun News*, July 2, 1967.

1955 aerial photo of the Organ Drive-In, on El Paseo Rd., just before the theater was renamed the Fiesta Drive-In. Courtesy Doña Ana County Community Development Department.

1974 aerial photo of the Fiesta Twin Drive-In. Originally the Organ Drive-In, the second screen was added in 1964. The indoor Video Twin Theater can be seen behind the original Organ screen. Courtesy Doña Ana County Community Development Department.

Marquee, Fiesta Drive-In, 1971. Note Academy Award Statuette. Courtesy
Estella Wilhelm.

Video Twin Theater showing the 1972 films YOUNG WINSTON and SOUNDER. Original screen of the Fiesta Drive-In shows behind the Video Twin. Courtesy Estella Wilhelm.

Taking down the original Organ screen of the Fiesta Drive-in to permit expanding the Video Twin into the Video Four, November, 1978. Courtesy Estella Wilhelm.

Concession and projection building, Fiesta Drive-In, July, 1978. Courtesy Estella Wilhelm.

1974 aerial photo of the Aggie Drive-In. The theater is bound on the south by Mahaney Dr. and on the east by N. Archuleta Rd. Courtesy Doña Ana County Community Development Department.

Marquee, Aggie Drive-In, 1991. Courtesy Estella Wilhelm.

Marquee, Aggie Drive-In, after the closing of the theater, 1993. Courtesy
Estella Wilhelm.

Concession and projection building, Aggie Drive-In, circa 1993. Courtesy
Estella Wilhelm.

Fire damage, concession and projection building, Aggie Drive-In. The building burned November 8, 1994. Courtesy Estella Wilhelm.

Abandoned screen and ticket booth, Aggie Drive-In, 1995. Courtesy Archives and
Special Collections, New Mexico State University.

Rio Grande Theater during Main Street refurbishing, 1996. Note the theater's drab appearance. Courtesy Archives and Special Collections, New Mexico State University.

Marquee, Rio Grande Theater, displaying U. S. MARSHALS, the theater's final showing before closing May 22, 1998. Courtesy Estella Wilhelm.

An unidentified employee posting the Rio Grande Theater's last public message, following the theater's final showing, May 22, 1998. Courtesy Estella Wilhelm.

Projector, Rio Grande Theater, May, 1998. Courtesy Estella Wilhelm.

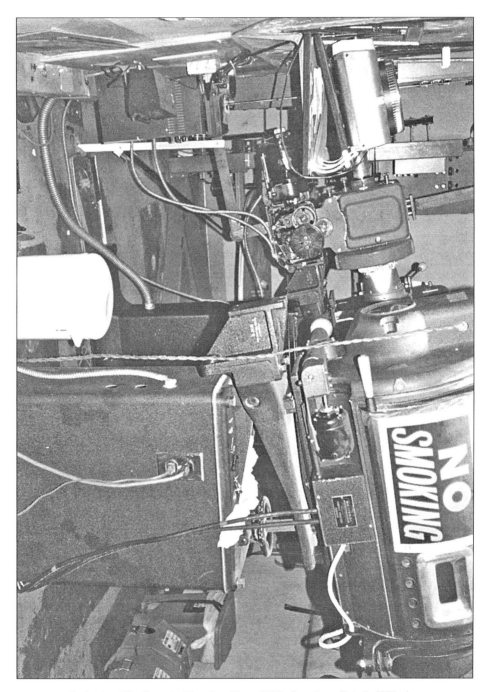

Projector, Rio Grande Theater, May, 1998. Courtesy Estella Wilhelm.

Restored Rio Grande Theater, 2007.

Restored iconic Rio Grande Theater marquee, 2007.

Restored Rio Grande Theater auditorium, 2007. Note "ghost light." (A "ghost light" is
a single bulb burning on a dark stage, an old English tradition.)

Rio Grande today, 2015. Las Cruces has spent millions to restore a downtown feel to Main Street. DAAC has spent millions to restore the Rio Grande Theater to its original Italian Renaissance Revival appearance. And yet Las Cruces town planners have almost totally hidden the theater from view by planting trees in front of it.

State Theater today, 2015. The city has planted a tree in front of it, hiding it from street view.

Theaters – 1906 - 2009

Rink Theater	
July, 1885	Albert Eugene Van Patten builds as skating rink and theater
July 27, 1907	Travelling company shows first movies

Vaudette Moving Picture Show	
February 15, 1908	Begins showing movies

Electric Theater (Grand, Bijou)	
May 23, 1908	Electric Theater opens in Armory Building
July 16, 1909	Name changes to Grand Theater
October 10, 1911	Name changes to Bijou

Wonderland Theater (Outdoor) (Airdome)	
February 2, 1909	Courtland O. Bennett and Park R. Birdwell open Wonderland Theater
March or April, 1909	Name changes to Airdome
October 4, 1912	Roline E. Banner buys theater
June, 1914	Banner closes Airdome and opens New Airdome

Crystal Theatre	
November 11, 1911	Crystal Theater opens
October, 1912	Roline E. Banner buys theater
1914	Crystal closes

Fountain of Pleasure Theater	
April, 1912	Albert J. Fountain, Jr. opens Fountain of Pleasure
April, 1916	Fountain goes out of business
September, 1919	Fountain re-opens
February 1, 1920	Fountain goes out of business
June 1, 1927	Fountain sells to Vicente D. Guerra
1938	Guerra sells theater back to Fountain
1951	Fountain closes
1963	Las Cruces Community Theater occupies Fountain
August, 1977	Las Cruces Community Theater moves to State Theater
September, 1977	Fountain resumes showing films
1989	Mesilla Valley Film Society occupies Fountain

Banner Theater (Star, A-muse-U, Navajo)	
September 12, 1913	Roline E. Banner opens Banner Theater
January, 1914	Name changes to Star, Bennett becomes partner
June, 1915	Banner buys out partner Bennett
January 21, 1916	Banner and Birdwell sell to Hanford and Cutis
January, 1916	Theater moves to Sam Bean Building
March 14, 1916	Star remodeled
May 16, 1916	Cutis buys out partner Hanford
June, 1916	Curtis sells to Birdwell
November 9, 1917	Birdwell sells to Emil Brutinel
August, 1919	Brutinel sells to Cupp & Sons
November, 1919	Cupp & Sons sells to R. W. Pierce
January 1, 1920	Pierce sells to Earl R. McMullen
February 26, 1920	Name changes to A-muse-U
May, 1922	McMullen sells to Charles D. Stewart
June, 1922	Name changes back to Star
September 21, 1922	Name changes to Navajo
October 18, 1924	Stewart sells to B. B. Hinman
October 24, 1924	Name changes back to Star
March 7, 1925	Hinman sells to J. F. Laubauch
June 4, 1927	Laubauch closes Star
July 23, 1927	Kohn and Fairchild Amusement Co buy Star
March 3, 1929	Star burns
August 24, 1929	Fox West Coast Theaters buys Star
October, 1929	Star closes

Open Air Picture Show (Outdoor)	
June 5, 1914	Banner opens Open Air Picture Show
June, 1915	Theater closes

New Airdome (Outdoor, Drive-In) (Movieland, Navajoland)	
July 11, 1914	Bennett and Birdwell open (new) Airdome Theater
June 29, 1915	Banner buys out partner Bennett
January 21, 1916	Banner and Birdwell sell to Hanford and Cutis
May, 1916	Cutis buys out partner Hanford
June, 1916	Curtis sells to Birdwell
November 9, 1917	Birdwell sells to Emil Brutinel
August, 1919	Brutinel sells to Cupp & Sons
November, 1919	Cupp & Sons sell to R. W. Pierce
January 1, 1920	Pierce sells to Earl R. McMullen
April, 1920	Name changes to Movieland

New Airdome (Outdoor, Drive-In) (Movieland, Navajoland)	
May, 1922	McMullen sells to Charles D. Stewart
May 9, 1923	Name changes to Navajoland
October 18, 1924	Stewart sells to B. B. Hinman
March 7, 1925	Hinman sells to J. F. Laubauch
April, 1925	Name changes back to Airdome
October 23, 1926	Laubauch closes Airdome

Theatre de Guadalupe (Outdoor, Drive-In) (De Luxe, Pastime)	
April 23, 1915	Wade Amusement Company opens Theatre de Guadalupe
May 11, 1915	Name changes to De Luxe Theater
June 29, 1915	Banner and Birdwell buy De Luxe Theater
June 13, 1916	Name changes to Pastime Theater
July, 1916	Pastime closes

Rio Grande Theater	
July 29, 1926	Central Theatres Corporation opens Rio Grande Theater
July 23, 1927	Kohn and Fairchild Amusement Co buy Rio Grande Theater
June 26, 1928	Wurlitzer organ installed
August 24, 1929	Fox West Coast Theaters buys Rio Grande
October 20, 1929	Rio Grande shows first talkie
April 7, 1930	William Fox forced out
October 25, 1930	First BILLY THE KID premier
July 28, 1933	Rio Grande burns
November 9, 1933	Rio Grande re-opens
May 28, 1935	Fox Theaters becomes Twentieth Century-Fox
May 29, 1941	Second BILLY THE KID premier
September 16, 1949	Rio Grande remodeled
April 14, 1954	Cinemascope installed
May 17, 1961	Rio Grande remodeled
June, 1982	Allen Theaters buys Rio Grande
May 22, 1998	Rio Grande closes
September 16, 2005	Doña Ana Arts Council acquires Rio Grande

Del Rio Theater (Plaza)	
February 22, 1930	Able Davis opens Del Rio Theater
January, 1931	Del Rio closes
August 3, 1933	Del Rio opens while Rio Grande is being repaired
November 9, 1933	Del Rio closes
December, 5, 1934	Del Rio burns
October 31, 1935	Fox Theaters opens repaired Del Rio

Del Rio Theater (Plaza)	
March 24, 1938	Name changes to Teatro Del Rio
April 7, 1939	Name changes back to Del Rio Theater
May 24, 1942	Del Rio remodeled
September 16, 1949	Name changes to Plaza Theater
December 8, 1952	Plaza burns
November 9, 1969	Plaza closes

Mission Theater (Park)	
May 11, 1937	Rod Bason opens Mission Theater
August, 1938	Bason sells to C. C. Dues
January 28, 1939	Dues sells to K. M. Davis
March, 1939	Mission closes
February 2, 1940	Fox Inter-Mountain Theaters re-opens Mission
January, 1941	Mission closes
August 6, 1944	S. E. and James Allen buy Mission
October 12, 1944	Mission re-opens
December, 1944	Mission closes
July 5, 1946	J. B. McMahon buys and opens Mission
March 14, 1947	McMahon sells to J. A. Weiss
September 23, 1960	Weiss estate sells to Fairmont Enterprises, Inc
September 23, 1960	Name changes to Park Theater
March 18, 1962	Park closes

State Theater	
December 21, 1941	Fox Inter-Mountain Theaters opens State Theater
September 16, 1949	State remodeled
August, 1977	Las Cruces Community Theater occupies State

Organ Drive-In (Fiesta)	
August 19, 1948	El Paso Amusement Company opens Organ Drive-In
January 16, 1955	Name changes to Fiesta
June, 1964	Fiesta gets a second screen
January 26, 1967	Video Independent Theaters, Inc. buys Fiesta
May 24, 1971	Original Organ screen replaced
December, 1978	Second screen removed for Video Twin expansion
February, 1981	Fiesta closed

Rocket Drive-In	
July 21, 1952	Hugh Cane opens Rocket Drive-In
November 28, 1965	Rocket closes

Aggie Drive-In (Aggie Twin)	
May 8, 1966	Lamar Gwaltney opens Aggie Drive-In
February 20, 1967	Video Independent Theaters, Inc buys Aggie
April, 1982	Gets second screen, becomes Aggie Twin
June, 1982	Allen Theaters buys Aggie Twin
1993	Aggie Twin closes

Video Twin Theaters (Video Four)	
March 10, 1972	Video Independent Theaters, Inc. opens Video Twin Theaters
June 29, 1979	Video Twin becomes Video Four
June, 1982	Allen Theaters buys Video Four

Cinema 4	
February 26, 1982	Video Independent Theaters, Inc. opens Cinema 4
June, 1982	Allen Theaters buys Cinema 4

Telshor Cinemas	
May 23, 1998	Allen Theaters opens Telshor Cinemas

Cineport 10 Theaters	
2009	Allen Theaters opens Cineport 10 Theaters

A CELEBRATED CASE
A FOOL THERE WAS
A SERPENTINE DANCE
ACROBATIC CLUB SWINGING
ADAM AND EVE
ANTOINE AND ANTOINETTE
BILLY THE KID
BULL FIGHT
CHARADE
COURAGE OF THE WEST
CREATURE OF THE JUNGLE
DIAMOND MASTER
DON JUAN
ESCAPE FROM ALCATRAZ
EYE FOR EYE
FARM SCENE
FOR A FEW DOLLARS MORE
FOREVER FEMALE
GARDEN OF EDEN
GERALDINE
HANG 'EM HIGH
HER BRIDAL NIGHT
HERCULE'S CAPTIVE WOMAN
HYPOCRITES
I'D RATHER BE RICH
JUDITH OF BETHULIA
JULIUS CAESAR
LA PALOMA
LAST TANGO IN PARIS
LOST HORIZON
LOVE SCENE
MARE NOSTRUM
MEET ME AT THE FOUNTAIN
MIDNIGHT COWBOY
MISTERIO DEL ROSTRO PALIDO
MONKEYSHINES NO 1
MONKEYSHINES NO 2
MOONRAKER
NERO
NUDE IN A WHITE CAR
OK DOCTOR
PASSIONNELLE
PIER AND WAVES
QUO VADIS,
ROCKY II,

SANTA FE
SEALED VERDICT
SIDEWALKS OF NEW YORK
SIEGFRIED
SOUNDER
TEN COMMANDMENTS
THE APPLE DUMPLING GANG RIDES
   AGAIN
THE AWFUL DR. ORLOF
THE BEST YEARS OF OUR LIVES
THE BIRTH OF A NATION
THE BRIDE IS MUCH TOO BEAUTIFUL
THE CHIMNEY SWEEP
THE DEEP PURPLE
THE DISCREET CHARM OF THE
   BOURGEOISIE
THE FALL OF BABYLON
THE FINDING OF AMERICA
THE FLYING FOOL
THE FOOTLIGHT PARADE
THE GREAT TRAIN ROBBERY
THE HORRIBLE DR. HICHCOCK
THE LOG JAM
THE LONGEST DAY
THE MILLION DOLLAR MYSTERY
THE OLD GERMAN MILL
THE OUTLAW
THE SECRET OF THE PURPLE REEF
THE SINGLE STANDARD
THE TEN BILLION DOLLAR VITAGRAPH
   MYSTERY
THE TIMBER QUEEN
THE TURNING POINT
THE TWENTY MILLION DOLLAR
   MYSTERY
THE WHITE GORILLA
THIS IS THE ARMY
TOO YOUNG TO KISS
TOP SERGEANT MILLIGAN
U. S. MARSHALS
VIVA MEXICO
WANTED A DOG
WAR PATH
YE HAUNTED WAYSIDE INN
YOUNG WINSTON

Notes

1 – Inventing Moving Pictures – A Brief History

1. John Edward Fletcher, *A Study of the Life and Works of Athanasius Kircher, 'Germanus Incredibilis': With a Selection of His Unpublished Correspondence and an Annotated Translation of His Autobiography* (Leiden and Boston, 2011), pp 143-144.

2. Charles Musser, *The Emergence of Cinema, History of the American Cinema, Vol. 1* (University of California Press, 1990), p 68.

3. Musser, *The Emergence of Cinema*, pp 62-63.

4. Musser, *The Emergence of Cinema*, pp 66.

5. Musser, *The Emergence of Cinema*, pp 71-72.

6. Musser, *The Emergence of Cinema*, p 71.

7. 'The Edison Kinetoscope,' *The Electrical Engineer, Vol. 18*, edited by A. C. Shaw (The Electrical Engineer, 1894), p 377.

8. Musser, *The Emergence of Cinema*, p 81.

9. Musser, *The Emergence of Cinema*, p 72.

10. Musser, *The Emergence of Cinema*, p 84.

11. Rémi Fournier Lanzoni, *French Cinema: From Its Beginnings to the Present* (Bloomsbury Publishing Inc, 2002), pp 14-17; Musser, *The Emergence of Cinema*, pp 135-137.

12. Douglas B. Thomas, *The Early History of German Motion Pictures, 1895-1935* (Thomas Intl., 1999), p 12.

13. Laurent Mannoni, *The Great Art Of Light And Shadow: Archaeology of the Cinema* (University of Exeter Press, 2000), pp 457-458.

14. John Barnes, *The Beginnings Of The Cinema In England, 1894-1901* (University of Exeter Press, 1998) pp 49-51.

15. Musser, *The Emergence of Cinema*, p 91.

16. Musser, *The Emergence of Cinema*, p 92.

17. *Sacramento Daily Record-Union*, September 27, 1896.

18. Musser, *The Emergence of Cinema*, pp 100-102.

19. Musser, *The Emergence of Cinema*, p 103.

20. Musser, *The Emergence of Cinema*, pp 109-111.

21. Musser, *The Emergence of Cinema*, p 112.

22. Deac Rossell, *Living Pictures: The Origins of the Movies* (State University of New York Press, 1998) pp 121-124.

23. Musser, *The Emergence of Cinema*, p 145.

24. Musser, *The Emergence of Cinema*, pp 145-148.

25. Raymond Fielding, *A Technological History of Motion Pictures and Television* (University of California Press, 1974) pp 4-5.

26. *The Phonoscope*, Vol. 1, No. 1 (The Phonoscope Publishing Company, 1896), p 10.

27. *The Phonoscope*, Vol. 1, No. 1, p 15.

28. *The Phonoscope*, Vol. 1, No. 10, p 13.

29. *Boston Post*, June 28, 1896.

30. *New York Times*, May 19, 1896.

31. *The Cincinnati Enquirer*, October 4, 1896.

32. *Brooklyn Daily Eagle*, March 23, 1897.

33. Musser, *The Emergence of Cinema*, pp 152, 226-227.

34. Musser, *The Emergence of Cinema*, p 166.

35. Musser, *The Emergence of Cinema*, p 168.

36. Musser, *The Emergence of Cinema*, p 232.

37. Siva Vaidhyanathan, *Copyrights and Copywrongs, The Rise of Intellectual Property and How It Threatens Creativity* (New York University Press, 2003), p 89.

38. Musser, *The Emergence of Cinema*, p 240.

39. *The Federal Reporter, Volume 110, Cases Argued and Determined in the Circuit Courts of Appeals and Circuit and District Courts of the United States*, October-November, 1901 (St. Paul West Publishing Co., 1901), pp 660-664.

40. *The Federal Reporter,* Volume 110, pp 664-665.

41. Musser, *The Emergence of Cinema,* p 305.

42. *The Sun* (NY), March 13, 1902.

43. Musser, *The Emergence of Cinema,* p 340.

44. Musser, *The Emergence of Cinema,* p 345.

45. *New York Daily Tribune,* February 28, 1900.

46. *The Brooklyn Daily Eagle,* May 2, 1900.

47. Jonathon Green, Nicholas J. Karolides, Reviser, *Encyclopedia of Censorship* (Facts on File, 1990) p 112.

48. D. M. Bennett, *Anthony Comstock, His Career of Cruelty and Crime* (Liberal and Scientific Publishing House, 1878), p 1016.

49. *The Brooklyn Daily Eagle,* September 30, 1888.

50. *The Daily Democrat* (Ohio), August 29, 1891.

51. *Altoona Mirror* (PA), March 13, 1906.

52. *The Charlotte News* (NC), September 27, 1906.

53. *Pittsburgh Daily Post,* October 27, 1907.

54. Eileen Bowser, *The Transformation of Cinema, History of the American Cinema,* Vol. 2 (University of California Press, 1990), pp 6-7.

55. Bowser, *The Transformation of Cinema,* p 27.

56. Bowser, *The Transformation of Cinema,* pp 84-95.

57. *New York Times,* July 16, 1912.

58. Bowser, *The Transformation of Cinema,* p 82.

59. Anthony Slide, Paul O'Dell, *Early American Cinema* (A. S. Barnes, 1970), p 62.

2 – Moving Pictures Arrive in Las Cruces

1. *El Paso Herald,* April 22, 1897.

2. *El Paso Herald,* April 23, 1897.

3. Musser, *The Emergence of Cinema,* p 78.

4. *El Paso Herald,* September 14, 1897.

5. *El Paso Herald,* December 27, 1897.

6. *El Paso Herald,* March 19, 1898.

7. *New York Dramatic Mirror,* June 24, 1899.

8. *El Paso Herald,* October 15, 1898.

9. *El Paso Herald,* August 29, 1899.

10. *El Paso Herald,* November 14, 1905.

11. *El Paso Herald,* November 14, 1905.

12. *El Paso Herald,* September 7, 1907.

13. *El Paso Herald,* October 28, 1907.

14. *El Paso Herald,* July 23, 1907.

15. *El Paso Herald,* January 24, 1908.

16. *Rio Grande Republican,* January 19, 1906.

17. Musser, *The Emergence of Cinema,* pp 354-355.

18. *Rio Grande Republican,* February 2, 1906.

19. *Rio Grande Republican,* July 27, 1907.

20. *Rio Grande Republican,* July 1, 1885.

21. *Rio Grande Republican,* August 12, 1907.

22. *El Paso Daily Herald,* June 4, 1897.

23. *Rio Grande Republican,* March 10, 1905.

24. *Rio Grande Republican,* December 12, 1908.

25. *Rio Grande Republican,* February 15, 1908.

26. *Rio Grande Republican,* March 7, 1908.

27. *Rio Grande Republican,* May 23, 1908.

28. *Rio Grande Republican,* June 27, 1908.

29. *Rio Grande Republican,* February 6, 1909.

30. *Rio Grande Republican,* June 30, 1911.

31. *Rio Grande Republican,* June 30, 1911.

32. *Rio Grande Republican,* July 16, 1909.

3 – Business Flourishes – 1909-1914

1. *The Springfield Daily Republican* (MO), May 16, 1909.

2. *The Springfield Daily Republican* (MO), May 16, 1909.

3. *The Atlanta Constitution,* August 19, 1909.

4. *El Paso Herald,* October 18, 1911.

5. *Rio Grande Republican,* October 13, 1911.

6. *Rio Grande Republican,* April 8, 1910.

7. *Rio Grande Republican,* October 24, 1911.

8. *Rio Grande Republican,* November 10, 1911.

9. *Rio Grande Republican,* October 10, 1911.

10. *Rio Grande Republican,* December 12, 1911.

11. *Rio Grande Republican,* February 16, 1912.

12. *Rio Grande Republican,* February 23, 1912.

13. *Rio Grande Republican,* June 17, 1898.

14. *Rio Grande Republican,* October 4, 1912.

15. *Rio Grande Republican,* October 28, 1912.

16. *Rio Grande Republican,* July 29, 1913.

17. *Rio Grande Republican,* September 12, 1913.

18. *Rio Grande Republican,* October 31, 1913.

19. *Rio Grande Republican,* November 25, 1913.

20. *Rio Grande Republican,* April 21, 1914.

21. *Rio Grande Republican,* June 5, 1914.

22. *Rio Grande Republican,* June 30, 1914.

23. *Rio Grande Republican,* July 10, 1914.

24. Richard M. Hollingshead, Jr., United States Patent number 1,909,537, May 16, 1933.

25. *El Paso Herald,* May 28, 1906.

26. *Tucumcari News and Times,* September 8, 1908.

27. *Rio Grande Republican,* February 6, 1909.

28. *Albuquerque Evening Herald,* May 2, 1911.

29. *Deming Headlight,* May 1, 1914.

30. *Deming Headlight,* May 22, 1914.

31. *Rio Grande Republic,* August 1, 1919.

32. *Rio Grande Republic,* December 1, 1914.

33. *The New Bern Sun* (NC), September 16, 1914.

34. *Rio Grande Republic,* December 1, 1914.

35. *The Ogden Standard* (UT), February 23, 1915.

36. *Harrisburg Telegraph* (PA), June 16, 1916.

37. *The Chicago Daily Tribune,* June 7, 1916.

38. Anthony Slide, *Inside the Hollywood Fan Magazine: A History of Star Makers, Fabricators, and Gossip Mongers* (University Press of Mississippi, 2010), p 121.

4 – War Years – 1915-1919

1. *Rio Grande Republican,* August 5, 1914.

2. *Rio Grande Republic,* April 16, 1915.

3. *Rio Grande Republic,* April 23, 1915.

4. *Rio Grande Republic,* April 27, 1915.

5. *Rio Grande Republic,* April 27, 1915.

6. *Rio Grande Republic,* May 11, 1915.

7. *Rio Grande Republic,* May 11, 1915.

8. *Rio Grande Republic,* June 29, 1915.

9. *Rio Grande Republic,* January 21, 1916.

10. *Rio Grande Republic,* January 21, 1916.

11. *Rio Grande Republic,* March 14, 1916.

12. *Rio Grande Republic,* May 16, 1916.

13. *Rio Grande Republican,* June 13, 1916.

14. *Rio Grande Republic,* June 30, 1916.

15. Richard Koszarski, *An Evening's Entertainment, History of the American Cinema,* Vol. 3 (University of California Press, 1990), pp 13-14.

16. *Rio Grande Republic,* July 7, 1916.

17. *Rio Grande Republic,* June 15, 1915.

18. Mark Garrett Cooper, *Universal Women: Filmmaking and Institutional Change in Early Hollywood* (University of Illinois Press, 2010), p 81.

19. Cooper, *Universal Women: Filmmaking and Institutional Change in Early Hollywood,* p 131.

20. *Rio Grande Republic,* December 1, 1916.

21. *Rio Grande Republic,* April 6, 1917.

22. *Rio Grande Republic,* April 3, 1917.

23. *Rio Grande Republic,* August 31, 1917.

24. *The Olean Evening Herald* (NY), October 29, 1917.

25. *Rio Grande Republic,* November 9, 1917.

26. *Rio Grande Republic,* January 18, 1918.

27. *Rio Grande Republic,* November 9, 1917.

28. *Rio Grande Republican,* Jan 25, 1918.

29. *Rio Grande Republican,* Jan 25, 1918.

30. *Rio Grande Republic,* May 31, 1918.

31. *Rio Grande Republic,* September 27, 1918.

32. *Rio Grande Republic,* November 15, 1918.

5 – The Twenties – 1920-1925

1. *El Paso Herald,* January 16, 1920.

2. *Rio Grande Republic,* December 18, 1919.

3. *Rio Grande Republic,* January 29, 1920.

4. *Rio Grande Republic,* February 26, 1920.

5. *Rio Grande Republic,* July 15, 1920.

6. *Rio Grande Republic,* May 20, 1920.

7. *Rio Grande Republic,* September 22, 1922.

8. *Rio Grande Republic,* May 18, 1922.

9. *Rio Grande Republic,* July 13, 1922.

10. *Rio Grande Republic,* Aug 17, 1922.

11. *Rio Grande Republic,* September 21, 1922.

12. *Rio Grande Republic,* November 16, 1922.

13. *Rio Grande Republic,* January 18, 1923.

14. Koszarski, *An Evening's Entertainment,* p 165.

15. *Rio Grande Republic,* Supplement, February 1, 1923.

16. *Rio Grande Farmer,* May 9, 1923.

17. *Las Cruces Citizen,* July 14, 1923.

18. *Las Cruces Citizen,* Sept 21, 1922.

19. *Rio Grande Farmer,* June 28, 1923.

20. *Las Cruces Citizen,* October 18, 1924.

21. *Las Cruces Citizen,* October 24, 1924.

22. *Las Cruces Citizen,* October 18, 1924.

23. *Las Cruces Citizen,* March 7, 1925.

24. *Las Cruces Citizen,* June 13, 1925.

25. *Las Cruces Citizen,* July 24, 1926.

6 – Coolest Place in the Valley – 1926-1929

1. J. F. Bonham, Guardian of Gertrude Martha Tucker and Sara Louise Tucker to C. T. Seale & B. G. Dyne, No. 53628, May 12, 1925, Doña Ana County Deed Book 70, p 52, Doña Ana County Courthouse.

2. *Rio Grande,* Doña Ana Arts Council, September 16, 2005.

3. *Las Cruces Citizen,* June 12, 1926.

4. *Las Cruces Citizen,* July 24, 1926.

5. *New York Times,* February 16, 1926.

6. Kendrick Scofield, "Spurlos Versenkt" in *Sea Power,* Vol. 6, January 1919 (Sea Powers Publishing Company, 1919), p 119.

7. *Las Cruces Citizen,* July 31, 1926.

8. *Las Cruces Citizen,* July 17, 1926.

9. *Las Cruces Citizen,* August 7, 1926.

10. *Las Cruces Citizen,* October 23, 1926.

11. *Las Cruces Citizen,* June 4, 1927.

12. *Las Cruces Citizen,* July 23, 1927.

13. *Las Cruces Citizen,* July 30, 1927.

14. *Las Cruces Citizen,* August 6, 1927.

15. *Las Cruces Citizen,* June 23, 1928.

16. *Estrella,* March 30, 1929.

17. *El Paso Herald,* August 24, 1929.

18. *Oakland Tribune* (CA), January 26, 1928.

19. *Las Cruces Citizen,* October 12, 1929.

20. *Las Cruces Citizen,* October 12, 1929.

21. "The Silent Drama," *Life Magazine,* Vol. 80, Issue 2075 (Life Publishing Company, 1922), p 24.

22. *Las Cruces Citizen,* October 12, 1929.

23. *Time Magazine,* Vol. XIV, No. 17, Oct. 21, 1929.

24. *Las Cruces Citizen,* October 19, 1929.

25. *Las Cruces Citizen,* October 19, 1929.

26. Tino Balio, *Grand Design: Hollywood as a Modern Business Enterprise, 1930-1939* (University of California Press, 1993), pp 13-14.

27. Eric L. Flom, *Chaplin in the Sound Era: An Analysis of the Seven Talkies* (McFarland & Co., 1997), p 50.

28. *The Brooklyn Daily Eagle* (NY), August 7, 1926.

29. *Arlington Heights Herald* (IL), October 22, 1926.

30. Flom, *Chaplin in the Sound Era: An Analysis of the Seven Talkies,* p 50.

31. Scott Eyman, *The Speed of Sound : Hollywood and the Talkie Revolution, 1926-1930* (Simon & Schuster, 1997), p 112.

7 – Depression Years – 1930-1939

1. "$400,000,000 May Come to Theatre," *Variety,* Vol. 108, No. 13, December 6, 1932 (Variety, 1932), p 7.

2. Tim McNeese, *The Great Depression 1929-1938* (Chelsea House, 2010.), p 39.

3. Sid Silverman, "What The Grosses Say," *Variety,* Vol. 105, No. 3, December 29, 1931 (Variety, 1931), p 3.

4. Tino Balio, *Grand Design: Hollywood as a Modern Business Enterprise, 1930-1939* (University of California Press, 1993), p 14.

5. *Las Cruces Citizen,* February 22, 1930.

6. *Las Cruces Citizen,* December 13, 1929.

7. Donald Crafton, *The Talkies: American Cinema's Transition to Sound, 1926-1931* (Scribner, 1997), p 87.

8. *Las Cruces Citizen,* November 22, 1930.

9. *Las Cruces Citizen,* October 4, 1930.

10. *Las Cruces Citizen,* October 25, 1930.

11. *Las Cruces Citizen,* Supplement, November 1, 1930.

12. *Silver City Independent* (NM), October 31, 1930.

13. *The Bend Bulletin* (OR), November 14, 1930.

14. *Oakland Tribune,* April 7, 1930.

15. *San Bernardino County Sun,* April 9, 1930.

16. *San Bernardino County Sun,* April 8, 1930.

17. *San Bernardino County Sun,* April 9, 1930.

18. *San Bernardino County Sun,* April 8, 1930.

19. Susan Fox, Donald G Rosellini, *William Fox: A Story of Early Hollywood, 1915-1930* (Midnight Marquee Press, 2006), pp 304-305.

20. *Las Cruces Citizen,* July 25, 1931.

21. *Las Cruces Citizen,* June 13, 1931.

22. *Las Cruces Citizen,* March 19, 1932.

23. *Las Cruces Citizen,* May 30, 1931.

24. *Las Cruces Citizen,* June 13, 1931.

25. *El Paso Herald-Post,* September 5, 1931.

26. *El Paso Herald Post,* September 9, 1931.

27. *Hamilton Daily News* (OH), June 20, 1932.

28. *Daily Journal-Gazette and Commercial-Star* (IL), July 29, 1932.

29. Roy Chartier, "Year in Pictures," *Variety,* Vol. 109, No. 4, January 3, 1933 (Variety, 1933), pp 2,48.

30. *Las Cruces Citizen,* July 20, 1933.

31. *El Paso Herald-Post,* July 29, 1933.

32. *El Paso Herald-Post,* August 4, 1933.

33. *Las Cruces Citizen,* August 3, 1933.

34. *Las Cruces Citizen,* October 26, 1933.

35. *Las Cruces Citizen,* August 3, 1933.

36. *Las Cruces Citizen,* November 9, 1933.

37. *Las Cruces Citizen,* November 2, 1933.

38. *El Paso Herald-Post,* December 12, 1934.

39. *Las Cruces Citizen,* December 6, 1934.

40. *Las Cruces Citizen,* October 31, 1935.

41. *Las Cruces Citizen,* March 24, 1938.

42. *Las Cruces Citizen,* March 24, 1938.

43. *Las Cruces Sun-News,* April 7, 1939.

44. *Las Cruces Sun-News,* May 5, 1939.

45. *Las Cruces Sun News,* July 2, 1939.

46. *El Paso Herald-Post,* July 20, 1938.

47. *El Paso Herald-Post,* July 20, 1938.

48. *El Paso Herald-Post,* July 20, 1938.

49. *San Bernardino County Sun* (CA), February 26, 1949.

8 – Mesilla and Mesilla Park

1. *Rio Grande Republican,* May 13, 1910.

2. *Rio Grande Republican,* May 13, 1910.

3. *Rio Grande Republican,* November 28, 1911.

4. *Rio Grande Republican,* December 8, 1911.

5. Home Mission Board of the Presbyterian Church to Albert J. Fountain [Jr.], August 23, 1905, Doña Ana County Deed Book 27, p 26, Doña Ana County Courthouse.

6. *Las Cruces Sun-News,* September 13, 1970.

7. Quirino Almeras to Albert J. Fountain Jr., August 9, 1890, Doña Ana County Deed Book 14, Part 1, pp 248-249, Doña Ana County Courthouse.

8. Business license, April 20, 1912, *Registration of Applications for Licenses for the County of Doña Ana,* p 27, Doña Ana County Courthouse.

9. *Polk's New Mexico and Arizona Pictorial State Gazetteer and Business Directory,* Vol. 1 (R. L. Polk & Co., 1912).

10. Business license, July 3, 1915, *Registration of Applications for Licenses for the County of Doña Ana,* p 37, Doña Ana County Courthouse.

11. Business license, September 8, 1919, *Registration of Applications for Licenses for the County of Doña Ana,* p 46, Doña Ana County Courthouse.

12. Albert J. Fountain [Jr.] and Theresa G. Fountain to Vicente D. Guerra and Winifred R. Guerra, June 1, 1927. Doña Ana County Deed Book 75, p 519, Doña Ana County Courthouse.

13. Business license, January 25, 1928, *Registration of Applications for Licenses for the County of Doña Ana,* p 71, Doña Ana County Courthouse

14. Business license, December 19, 1929, *Registration of Applications for Licenses for the County of Doña Ana,* p 79, Doña Ana County Courthouse

15. The History of the Fountain Theatre web site: www.mesillavalleyfilm.org/the_history_of_the_fountain_theatre.php.

16. The History of the Fountain Theatre web site: www.mesillavalleyfilm.org/the_history_of_the_fountain_theatre.php.

17. *Las Cruces Sun-News,* March 9, 1972.

18. *Las Cruces Sun-News,* November 24, 1965.

19. *Las Cruces Sun-News,* November 24, 1965.

20. *Las Cruces Sun-News,* February 26, 1974.

21. *Las Cruces Sun-News,* September 11, 1977.

22. Las Cruces Sun-News, July 26, 1978

23. Las Cruces Sun-News, October 10, 1978

24. Las Cruces Sun-News, May 17, 1979

25. The History of the Fountain Theatre web site: www.mesillavalleyfilm.org/the_history_of_the_fountain_theatre.php.

26. *Las Cruces Sun-News,* March 12, 1970.

27. *Las Cruces Sun-News,* April 6, 1976.

28. *Las Cruces Citizen,* May 13, 1937.

29. *Las Cruces Sun,* November 19, 1937.

30. *Las Cruces Citizen,* March 3, 1938.

31. *Las Cruces Sun-News,* February 1, 1940.

32. *Las Cruces Sun-News,* April 13, 1939.

33. *Las Cruces Sun-News,* November 6, 1939.

34. *Las Cruces Sun-News,* March 12, 1939.

35. *Las Cruces Sun-News,* November 6, 1939.

9 – The Forties – 1940-1949

1. *Las Cruces Sun-News,* February 1, 1940.

2. *Las Cruces Sun-News,* March 13, 1941.

3. *Las Cruces Sun-News,* March 9, 1941.

4. Robert M. Utley, *Billy the Kid, A Short and Violent Life* (University of Nebraska Press, 1989), pp 203-204.

5. *Las Cruces Sun-News,* April 4, 1941.

6. *Las Cruces Sun-News,* May 23, 1941.

7. *Las Cruces Sun News,* March 9, 1947.

8. *Las Cruces Sun-News,* May 30, 1941.

9. *Las Cruces Sun-News,* May 30, 1941.

10. *Las Cruces Sun-News,* May 30, 1941.

11. *Las Cruces Sun-News,* June 20, 1941.

12. *Las Cruces Sun-News,* September 12, 1941.

13. *Las Cruces Sun-News,* September 11, 1941.

14. *Las Cruces Sun-News,* December 8, 1941.

15. *Las Cruces Sun-News,* December 21, 1941.

16. *Las Cruces Sun-News,* December 21, 1941.

17. *Las Cruces Sun-News,* December 21, 1941.

18. *Las Cruces Sun-News,* December 21, 1941.

19. *Las Cruces Sun-News,* December 26, 1941.

20. *Las Cruces Sun-News,* December 21, 1941.

21. *Las Cruces Sun-News,* December 21, 1941.

22. *Las Cruces Sun-News,* April 16, 1942.

23. *Las Cruces Sun-News,* May 24, 1942.

24. *Las Cruces Sun-News,* December 1, 1942.

25. *Las Cruces Sun-News,* December 2, 1942.

26. Laurence Bergreen, "Irving Berlin, This Is The Army," *Prologue Magazine,* Vol. 28, No. 2., Summer, 1996, www.archives.gov/publications/prologue/1996/summer/irving-berlin-1.html.

27. *Las Cruces Sun-News,* October 17, 1943.

28. *Las Cruces Sun-News,* October 22, 1943.

29. Bergreen, "Irving Berlin, This Is The Army."

30. *Las Cruces Sun-News,* August 6, 1944.

31. *Las Cruces Sun-News,* October 12, 1944.

32. *Las Cruces Sun-News,* December 1, 1944.

33. *Las Cruces Sun-News,* May 8, 1945.

34. *Las Cruces Sun-News,* September 2, 1945.

35. *Las Cruces Sun-News,* March 14, 1947.

36. *Las Cruces Sun-News,* October 4, 1948.

37. *Las Cruces Sun-News,* June 25, 1948.

38. *Las Cruces Sun-News,* August 19, 1948.

39. *Las Cruces Sun-News,* August 19, 1948.

40. *Las Cruces Sun-News,* April 19, 1949.

41. *Las Cruces Citizen,* August 9, 1949.

42. *Las Cruces Citizen,* March 21, 1950.

43. *Las Cruces Sun-News,* September 18, 1949.

10 – Fifties and Beyond

1. Thomas Schatz, Boom and Bust: American Cinema in the 1940s (Scribner, 1997) pp 329-330.

2. Kerry Segrave, Drive-in Theaters: A History from Their Inception in 1933 (McFarland & Co., 1992), pp 13-14.

3. Las Cruces Sun-News, June 26, 1950.

4. Robert Leckie, Conflict: The History of the Korean War, 1950-53 (Putnam, 1962), p68.

5. Las Cruces Sun-News, June 30, 1950.

6. Las Cruces Sun-News, May 24, 1953.

7. Las Cruces Sun-News, May 14, 1952.

8. Las Cruces Sun-News, July 21, 1952.

9. Las Cruces Sun-News, July 21, 1952.

10. Las Cruces Sun-News, December 8, 1952.

11. Las Cruces Sun-News, December 8, 1952.

12. Las Cruces Sun-News, September 23, 1953.

13. Las Cruces Sun-News, April 14, 1954.

14. El Paso Herald-Post, September 26, 1952.

15. Las Cruces Sun-News, July 12, 1954.

16. Las Cruces Sun-News, July 26, 1954.

17. Las Cruces Sun-News, September 26, 1954.

18. Las Cruces Sun-News, January 16, 1955.

19. Las Cruces Sun-News, September 23, 1960.

20. Las Cruces Sun-News, March 18, 1962.

21. Las Cruces Sun-News, April 24, 1962.

22. Las Cruces Sun-News, May 16, 1961.

23. Las Cruces Sun-News, May 16, 1961.

24. Las Cruces Sun-News, December 8, 1961.

25. Las Cruces Sun-News, May 4, 1966.

26. Las Cruces Sun-News, May 4, 1966.

27. Las Cruces Sun-News, May 8, 1966.

28. Las Cruces Sun-News, May 28, 1982.

29. Las Cruces Sun-News, May 25, 1967.

30. Las Cruces Sun-News, May 25, 1967.

31. Las Cruces Sun-News, May 25, 1967.

32. Howard Hughes, Aim For the Heart, The Films of Clint Eastwood (I. B. Tauris & Co Ltd, 2009) p 18.

33. Las Cruces Sun-News, June 12, 1967.

34. Las Cruces Sun-News, June 21, 1967.

35. Las Cruces Sun-News, June 29, 1967.

36. Las Cruces Sun-News, June 28, 1967.

37. Las Cruces Sun-News, June 29, 1967.

38. Las Cruces Sun-News, July 2, 1967.

39. Hughes, p 18.

40. Las Cruces Sun-News, June 28, 1968.

41. Las Cruces Sun-News, February 12, 1970.

42. Las Cruces Sun-News, May 6, 1970.

43. Las Cruces Sun-News, June 3, 1964.

44. Las Cruces Sun-News, November 28, 1965.

45. Las Cruces Sun-News, February 20, 1967.

46. Las Cruces Sun-News, April 26, 1971.

47. Las Cruces Sun-News, Supplement, April 28, 1971.

48. Las Cruces Sun-News, March 9, 1972.

49. Las Cruces Sun-News, January 24, 1972.

50. Las Cruces Sun News, June 11, 1978

51. Las Cruces Sun News, June 11, 1978

52. Las Cruces Sun-News, December 12, 1978

53. Las Cruces Sun News, June 29, 1979

54. Las Cruces Sun-News, July 14, 1997.

55. Las Cruces Sun-News, June 11, 1982.

56. Las Cruces Sun-News, February 26, 1982.

57. Las Cruces Sun-News, May 23, 1998.

58. Las Cruces Sun-News, May 22, 1998.

59. Rio Grande Theater, Doña Ana Arts Council program, September 16, 2005

Index

Doc45 Publications

La Posta – From the Founding of Mesilla, to Corn Exchange Hotel, to Billy the Kid Museum, to Famous Landmark, David G. Thomas, paperback, 118 pages, 59 photos, e-book available.

"For someone who grew up in the area of Mesilla, it's nice to have a well-researched book about the area – and the giant photographs don't hurt either.... And the thing I was most excited to see is a photo of the hotel registry where the name of "William Bonney" is scrawled on the page.... There is some debate as to whether or not Billy the Kid really signed the book, which the author goes into, but what would Billy the Kid history be without a little controversy?" –Billy the Kid Outlaw Gang Newsletter, Winter, 2013.

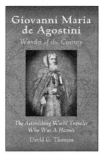

Giovanni Maria de Agostini, Wonder of The Century – The Astonishing World Traveler Who Was A Hermit, David G. Thomas, paperback, 208 pages, 59 photos, 19 maps, e-book available.

"David G. Thomas has finally pulled back the veil of obscurity that long shrouded one of the most enduring mysteries in New Mexico's long history to reveal the true story of the Hermit, Giovanni Maria de Agostini. ...Thomas has once again proven himself a master history detective. Of particular interest is the information about the Hermit's life in Brazil, which closely parallels his remarkable experience in New Mexico, and required extensive research in Portuguese sources. Thomas's efforts make it possible to understand this deeply religious man." – Rick Hendricks, New Mexico State Historian

Torpedo Squadron Four – A Cockpit View of World War II, Gerald W. Thomas, paperback, 280 pages, 209 photos, e-book available.

"This book contains more first-person accounts than I have seen in several years. ...we can feel the emotion... tempered by the daily losses that characterized this final stage of the war in the Pacific. All in all, one of the best books on the Pacific War I have seen lately." – Naval Aviation News, Fall 2011.

Made in the USA
San Bernardino, CA
30 December 2015